■SCHOLASTIC

MEMORIZING STRATEGIES

& OTHER BRAIN-BASED ACTIVITIES

That Help Kids Learn, Review, and Recall

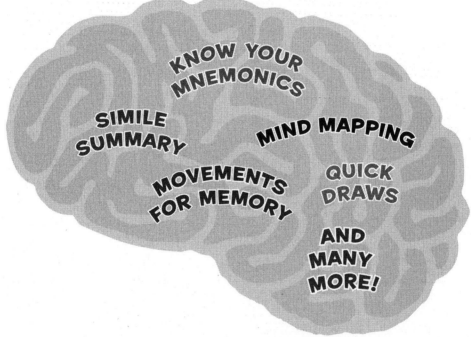

KNOW YOUR MNEMONICS

SIMILE SUMMARY

MIND MAPPING

MOVEMENTS FOR MEMORY

QUICK DRAWS

AND MANY MORE!

by LeAnn Nickelsen

NEW YORK • TORONTO • LONDON • AUCKLAND • SYDNEY
MEXICO CITY • NEW DELHI • HONG KONG • BUENOS AIRES

Teaching *Resources*

DEDICATION

Thank You . . .

To Joel, my husband of 11 years, who is my best friend

To Keaton and Aubrey, my 4-year-old twins, who bring excitement and joy to my life

To Jim and Dolores Heim, my parents, who have always been there for me

*To Eric Jensen, my brain-research mentor and author of 25 books about the brain,
for being the best resource. Your books and knowledge are invaluable to me.
Thank you for your help in refining the brain-research facts within this book.*

*To Virginia Dooley and Maria L. Chang, my editors, for your incredible writing ability,
wealth of ideas, and the opportunity to publish once more*

*To all of the educators and districts that I have worked with on a regular
basis and presented to. I appreciate all of your feedback and ideas:*

*Grapevine-Colleyville, TX
Olathe, KS
Gardner-Edgerton, KS
West Chester, OH (Lakota)
Waynesville, OH
Perth Amboy, NJ
Pennsylvania school districts*

*To Linda Allen and Deborah Tapp—
what great brain-based M&M's you are!*

Cover design by James Sarfati
Interior design by Holly Grundon
Illustrations by Patricia Wynne and Marcy Ramsey

ISBN 0-439-21560-9
Copyright © 2004 by LeAnn Nickelsen
All rights reserved.
Printed in the U.S.A.

7 8 9 10   40   11 10 09 08

CONTENTS

"Education is discovering the brain, and that's about the best news there could be.... Anyone who does not have a thorough, holistic grasp of the brain's architecture, purpose and main ways of operating is as far behind the times as an automobile designer without a full understanding of engines."

— LESLIE HART

In these days of standardized testing, students are expected to learn AND retain more information than ever before. With so much information bombarding students' brains, how can you make sure that they hold on to the important facts, theories, and ideas that they need not only to succeed on tests but also to help their knowledge base grow?

This book can help! *Memorizing Strategies & Other Brain-Based Activities That Help Kids Learn, Review, and Recall* starts by giving you an overview of how the brain works, including the latest in brain research, written in easy-to-understand language. We even provide an analogy, called the Learning Trip, to explain how the brain sifts through incoming information and decides what's important enough to store in long-term memory. With this base, we then provide practical, classroom-tested strategies for helping students learn and memorize the information they need to

> **"When laughter and education work together, expect everything."**
>
> —DIANE LOOMANS

know. You'll find a variety of quick activities you can do during and at the end of a lesson, as well as several fun and engaging review games students can play every week to help cement information into their brains. Finally, at the back of this book, you'll find 25 surefire tips to help students make the most of their study time. Please feel free to photocopy and distribute these study pages to all your students.

Enjoy!

What This Book Will Do for You, the TEACHER:

This book will provide you with

- the knowledge of how the brain works;
- the research behind reviewing;
- the knowledge of when to review information;
- five powerful techniques that enhance reviewing;
- ten fun, easy-to-use review games for any content;
- teacher instructions, student instructions, and student reproducibles for each review game.

What This Book Will Do for the STUDENT:

This book will provide each student with

- strategies for recalling information more quickly;
- summarizing strategies to use during processing time;
- questioning techniques to improve review;
- ways to make information more meaningful, thus more memorable;
- excitement while playing game to review content;
- rubrics to help learn the social graces that come with playing games;
- clear instructions and reproducibles to use for each game;
- study guidelines that will enhance home reviewing for tests.

CHAPTER 1

HOW THE BRAIN WORKS

"It is shameful for a man to rest in ignorance of the structure of his own body, especially when the knowledge of it mainly conduces to his welfare, and directs his application of his own powers."

—PHILIPP MELANCHTHON

GETTING TO KNOW THE BRAIN

The brain is the body's control center, responsible for monitoring and regulating breathing and heart rate, dealing with emotions, coordinating movement, analyzing and processing information, and so much more! In this chapter, we'll look specifically at eight parts of the brain that work together to manage learning and memory:

 1 RETICULAR ACTIVATING SYSTEM (RAS):
The RAS "serves as an effective filter for the thousands of stimuli constantly bombarding the sensory receptors, allowing you to focus on relevant stimuli. It excludes background information and tunes out distractions or trivial sensory information" (Wolfe, 2001). Located in the brain stem, the RAS regulates the amount and type of sensorimotor information allowed into the brain, then forwards the information to the thalamus. The RAS is important to the review process because students can't learn what you are teaching unless they are paying attention, and the RAS regulates what the brain pays attention to.

PARTS OF THE BRAIN

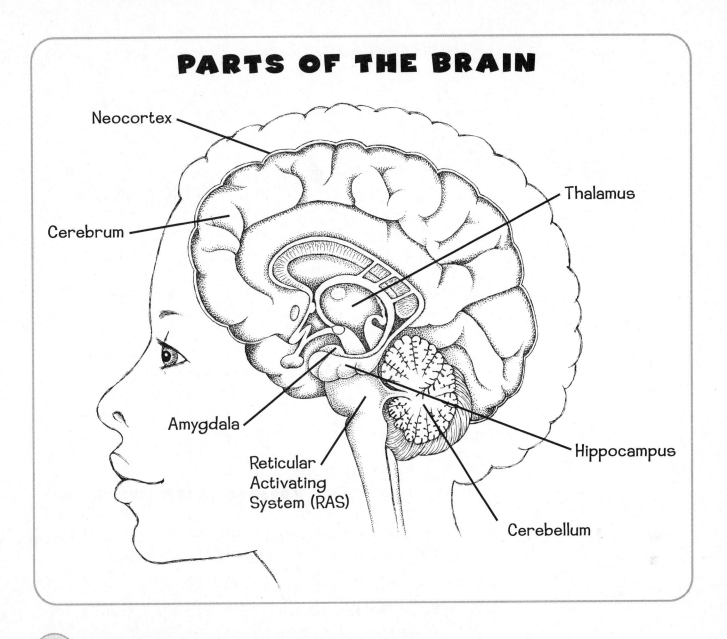

2 **THALAMUS:** This part of the brain sorts information and sends it to the appropriate places within the brain for processing. For example, if visual information is being sent, the thalamus will send it to the occipital lobe, the visual-processing part of the brain. The thalamus is important to the review process because it sends information to the proper places in the brain so that processing can occur.

3 **CEREBRUM:** Composed of the left and right hemispheres, the cerebrum makes up 85 percent of the brain's mass. It controls sensory interpretation, thinking, and memory, and is the place for thinking and decision making. Information allowed into the brain is taken apart, rebuilt, and connected to other information in the cerebrum. Reviewing is a great way to strengthen neural connections that exist within the brain.

AMYGDALA: While the thalamus is sending information to the cortex or cerebrum, it is also sending the same information to the amygdala, the seat of emotion. Information that has emotion tied to it is more likely to make it to long-term storage because strong emotions trigger the release of noradrenaline, a memory fixative. This noradrenaline can act as a cement and lock in the information. "Emotions drive the threesome of attention, meaning, and memory. The things that we orchestrate to engage emotions in a productive way will do 'triple duty' to capture all three" (Jensen, 1998). The review games in Chapter 5 are designed to generate excitement—a great way to reinforce key information in students' brains.

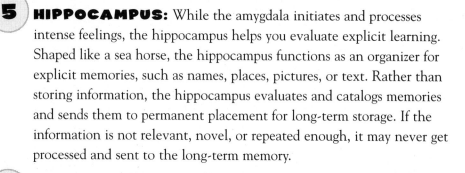 **HIPPOCAMPUS:** While the amygdala initiates and processes intense feelings, the hippocampus helps you evaluate explicit learning. Shaped like a sea horse, the hippocampus functions as an organizer for explicit memories, such as names, places, pictures, or text. Rather than storing information, the hippocampus evaluates and catalogs memories and sends them to permanent placement for long-term storage. If the information is not relevant, novel, or repeated enough, it may never get processed and sent to the long-term memory.

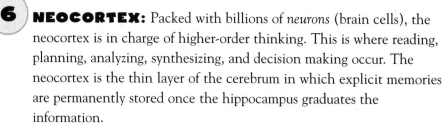 **NEOCORTEX:** Packed with billions of *neurons* (brain cells), the neocortex is in charge of higher-order thinking. This is where reading, planning, analyzing, synthesizing, and decision making occur. The neocortex is the thin layer of the cerebrum in which explicit memories are permanently stored once the hippocampus graduates the information.

CEREBELLUM: This part of the brain resembles a little bell or miniature brain and controls movement. Baseball superstar Alex Rodriguez's cerebellum helps coordinate his muscles perfectly to swing the bat and smash the ball over the fence or snare line drives. Olympic gymnasts' cerebellums are wired for balance, back flips, and so on. Movement is a powerful way to cement information into long-term memory (Jensen, 2000). See "Movements for Memory," page 23, for suggestions on how you can incorporate movement into your lessons.

 NEURONS: These small but powerful brain cells transmit messages to and from the brain to the rest of the body. A *stimulus* (e.g., a piece of data or the smell of smoke) causes nerve impulses to travel through a neuron, starting at the *dendrite*. The dendrite receives the message or stimulus and sends it to the cell body and then to the whiplike *axon*. When the electrical impulse triggers the release of chemicals, or *neurotransmitters*, at the end of the axon, it is transmitted to the next neuron across a small gap called the *synapse*. Receptors located on the surface of the dendrite of the next neuron takes certain chemicals and continues the same process until the chemical information reaches its destination within the brain. This sequence of neural firings forms a pattern of neural connections. Reviewing strengthens existing connections and adds more neural links to the network of neurons. The stronger the connections are between neurons, the faster and easier the information can be retrieved.

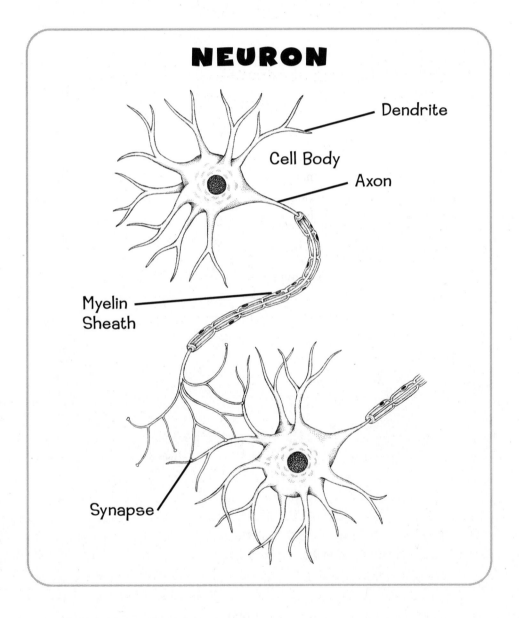

NEURON

Dendrite

Cell Body

Axon

Myelin Sheath

Synapse

"The student who can begin early in life to see things as connected has begun the life of learning. The connectedness of things is what the educator contemplates to the limit of his/her capacity."

—MARK VAN DOREN

Now that we've explored the different parts of the brain that affect learning and memory, let's look at a simple visual representation of how information goes from short-term memory to long-term memory.

THE LEARNING TRIP

The Learning Trip model below, based on a model by brain expert David Sousa, is a simple symbolic representation of how the brain learns information and how memories are formed. The terms used in this model are convenient labels that help illustrate the process the brain goes through to properly receive, review, and retrieve information. Keep in mind that each brain is unique and may experience different results in one or more stages of this Learning Trip.

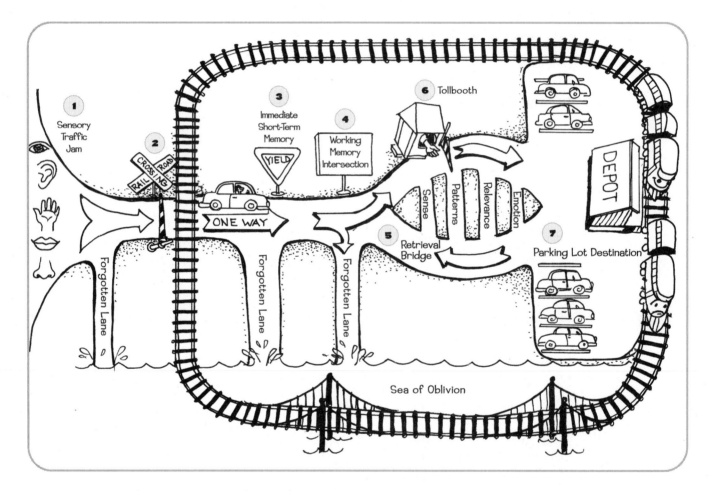

1 SENSORY TRAFFIC JAM (SENSORY INPUT STAGE)

The journey starts with a "jam" of information; tens of thousands of bits of sensory information (i.e., seeing, hearing, touching, smelling, tasting) bombard the brain per second. Fortunately, the brain has a built-in filter that allows it to focus only on what is important to that particular brain. (See "Receiving Information," p. 13, for tips on how to make sure important information is encoded accurately and meaningfully into students' brains.)

2 RAILROAD CROSSING (FILTERING STAGE)

The RAS (reticular activating system) and the thalamus work together at this stage of the Learning Trip. When the safety rail at the Railroad Crossing is down, little or no information can get past the RAS; when the rail is up, information can go through and the thalamus sends it on to its designated spot in the brain for processing. This safety rail determines what the brain pays attention to. The amount the rail opens or closes depends on how the brain perceives the incoming information. A person's long-term memory, with all its prior knowledge and past experiences, can affect whether or not the brain focuses on or pays attention to the information. For example, if information that has been previously associated with failure (sad train from the Parking Lot Destination) arrives at the Railroad Crossing, it may evoke feelings of anger, frustration, or helplessness. The information may not go further. (A student may tune out math, for instance, if he has previously failed in math.) The safety rail will open, on the other hand, when successful memories and experiences (happy train) evoke good, receptive feelings. (A student will most likely pay attention to a writing lesson if she has felt success with writing.)

3 YIELD SIGN (IMMEDIATE SHORT-TERM MEMORY)

At this stage, information pauses at a yield sign for about 15 to 30 seconds while the brain makes a decision: Is this information important enough to take to long-term storage or is it something that can be forgotten? For example, you may need to remember a phone number long enough to dial it, but afterwards it can pass down to Forgotten Lane.

4 WORKING MEMORY INTERSECTION (SHORT-TERM WORKING MEMORY)

This part of the trip (representing the brain's frontal lobes) is a type of short-term memory, but the brain focuses on the information here much longer than in immediate short-term memory. This is where the brain builds, takes apart, and reworks information, and links it to past experiences and knowledge (see "Retrieval Bridge"). The frontal lobe is the conscious part of the brain, hard at work when a person is conversing, writing, reading, or listening. If the topic is interesting or there is a sense of responsibility attached to the information (for example, the brain is aware that this information will be on an upcoming test), its stay may be extended at this intersection.

5 RETRIEVAL BRIDGE

Information from the Parking Lot Destination, or long-term storage (i.e., past experiences and prior knowledge), travels over the Retrieval Bridge to connect to the new information. In order for new information to be remembered, it must be relevant—in other words, it must connect to something similar that's already stored in the brain. Novelty gets our attention while familiarity helps us make meaning. This is why comparing and contrasting strategies—as well as sorting, metaphors, similes, and analogies—are so important for memory. (See "Simile Summary," page 19.)

6 TOLLBOOTH (SENSE + MEANING = CONNECTIONS)

This Tollbooth allows information through only if the "fee" is paid—that is, if the information makes sense, follows a familiar pattern, is relevant, or has an emotional link attached to it. (In other words, the Retrieval Bridge was activated and information from the Parking Lot Destination meets up with the new incoming information at the Tollbooth.) If the new information meets any of these criteria, it can go through the Tollbooth and be stored in the Parking Lot Destination. If the fee is not paid—the new information does not make sense or has no meaning attached to it—it eventually turns down Forgotten Lane.

You can help new information get past students' "Tollbooth" by:

◎ helping students see a pattern in the information or connect it to something they already know, so it can be linked to prior knowledge. (See "Summarizing Success," page 28.)

◎ helping students understand why they need to learn this information. How is this information relevant to their personal lives?

◎ associating the information with a particular emotion. Emotions are highly remembered.

7 PARKING LOT DESTINATION (LONG-TERM STORAGE)

This is the goal—long-term storage! How do you know if information made it into long-term storage? Give students a test or quiz 24 hours later (with no review). If they score well, then they probably understood the information and have it stored in long-term storage. If you want the information to remain there even longer, then you must keep reviewing it. Information that is not reviewed regularly could eventually wind up on Forgotten Lane. Tests should continue to review the most important information from previous learning units. Having the information appear in tests, review games, and daily lessons in an active, fun way will help students remember the information.

CHAPTER 2

FROM LEARNING TO MEMORIZING

> " Memory is like a piece of music—it has lots of different parts that come together to create the whole. "
>
> —MARCU RAICHLE

New information is most likely to make it to long-term storage when three processes occur:

1. **the information is received correctly;**
2. **the information is reviewed correctly; and**
3. **the information is retrieved correctly.**

In this chapter you will find some strategies to help incoming information or stimuli become a memory that will last.

RECEIVING INFORMATION

To ensure that information is received and encoded accurately and meaningfully into students' brains, try to present the information in different manners—visually, auditorily, and kinesthetically—so that you reach students of different learning styles. Provide opportunities for students to make the information meaningful for themselves. One example would be to activate students' prior knowledge; in other words, connect the new information with something they already know. For example, if you're having a discussion about prejudice, you might ask, *"Have any of you ever felt that you were treated unfairly because you were different in some way?"* Encourage students to share personal experiences. Then explain, *"What you just shared with the class are examples of dealing with somebody with a prejudiced attitude."*

REVIEWING INFORMATION

For information to make it into long-term memory it must be maintained or strengthened over time through rote or elaborative review—use it or lose it. Reviewing does the following for our *neural networks* (groups of neurons that fire together when a particular stimuli is recognized):

1. It adds more connections to already existing neural pathways through elaborative review.
2. It produces strong connections between neurons so the neural pathway can be easily accessed when needed.

ROTE VS. ELABORATIVE REVIEW

Review can mean repeating the exact same information over and over until it can be easily recalled. This is called *rote review* or *rote rehearsal*, and retention is highly likely. Examples of rote review include repeating the alphabet, song lyrics, and multiplication tables. Rote rehearsal, however, doesn't give the learner opportunities for deeper meaning and elaboration.

Elaborative review is a "broad category encompassing a variety of strategies" (Wolfe, 2001) that helps students elaborate on a topic in such a way that enhances understanding, meaning, relevance, and retention of that information. One way to help students attach greater sense and meaning to new information is to provide processing time. Allot enough time for students to talk to one another about a particular topic so they can process the information as well as hear other people's perspectives. (See "Super Sleuth Review," page 24, for example.) Processing information includes paraphrasing, reorganizing, questioning, summarizing, and so on.

With elaborative review, more connections are made and larger neural networks are being formed. Here is an example of how elaboration makes neural networks stronger:

> **Students were taught the difference between** *weather* **and** *climate*. **They processed the information within a group by giving examples of climate and weather:**
>
> "I visited the Bahamas last year. The climate there was tropical. It was pretty hot and humid, but breezy."
>
> "The stormy weather over the weekend scared me at night because the thunder was so loud."

Not only were these comments meaningful and relevant to students—more details were added to their existing neural networks on weather and climate.

> **"** The more fully we process information over time, the more connections we make, the more consolidation takes place, and the better the memory will be. **"**
>
> —PAT WOLFE

The great benefit of elaboration is that when any of the concepts is reintroduced, the whole network is strengthened. Rehearsal is so important because it strengthens the neural network, making it easier to recall information.

CREATING STRONGER CONNECTIONS

On page 8, we describe how neurons work and fire together to form a network. Reviewing bolsters newly formed networks. In his book *How the Brain Learns*, David Sousa describes how neural networks become stronger: "The firing may last only for a brief time, after which the memory decays and is lost. If the second neuron (within the network) is not stimulated again, it will stay in a state of readiness for hours or days."

It is during this state of readiness that information needs to be repeated through practice or rehearsal in order to increase the chances of a neural network's survival. Eventually, repeated firing of the pattern binds the neurons together so that if one fires, the whole network fires, forming a new memory trace (or *engram*). Imagine forging a path through the woods. The first time you walk through it, the going is hard and slow. But each time you travel along the path, it becomes easier and quicker to walk through. Similarly, the more a neural network is used (through repeated review of information), the faster and easier it will be to retrieve the information.

RETRIEVING INFORMATION

Information that is associated powerfully in the brain is more likely to be retrieved easily. One of the best ways to help students remember information is to link it to prior information. An association or a cue to the information can automatically trigger its retrieval. Mnemonics is one example of using a cue to retrieve information. For example, the mnemonic, *"When two vowels go walking, the first one does the talking,"* can help children remember how to decode the word *teach*. (See "Know Your Mnemonics," page 26, for more examples.)

SUMMARY

To enhance students' memory, make sure that you impart information in ways that reach different learning styles and that you offer opportunities for the information to become meaningful. Then, review the information again and again so that networks are strengthened, making the retrieval process easier.

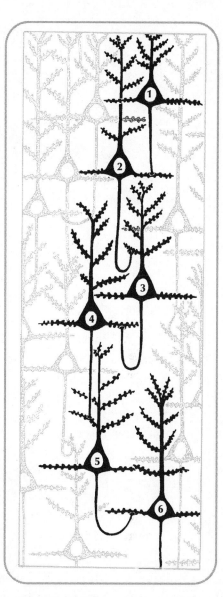

Reviewing helps create and strengthen a potential neural network. When a stimulus sets off a neuron, this in turn can set off a second neuron. If neuron 1 soon fires again (through review or rehearsal), a connection is formed between neurons 1 and 2. The next time neuron 1 is stimulated, no matter how weakly, neuron 2 will be set off. This may continue to happen with neurons 3, 4, and so on until a neural network is formed. If neuron 1 is not fired again (or reviewed) soon, then the link between neuron 1 and neuron 2 is not strong enough to form a neural network.

CHAPTER 3

BEST TIMES FOR REVIEW

> "As we remember, we etch lines and patterns in the soft surface; then time—the great eraser—slowly smooths the lines away, causing us to forget."
>
> —PLATO

 elieve it or not, there are some "prime times" when the brain is more susceptible to receiving and processing information. During these times, reviewing can be more effective and more powerful. The key is knowing when these times are and how to take advantage of them.

MASSED AND DISTRIBUTED PRACTICE (10-24-7)

Madeline Hunter, author of *Elements of Effective Instruction*, suggests that teachers use two types of practice over time to strengthen students' memories: massed practice and distributed practice.

Massed practice occurs when students review new learning at close time intervals to strengthen neural connections. If information is not rehearsed right away, it can quickly fade. An example of massed practice is cramming for a test. Material is quickly chunked into working memory. However, once the test is taken and if the information isn't reviewed again, much of it will be forgotten unless students take the time to make the information meaningful. "Practice that is distributed over longer periods of time sustains meaning and consolidates the learning into long-term storage in a form that will ensure accurate recall and applications in the future" (Sousa, 2001).

Distributed practice helps ensure that information is retained for a much longer period of time. In distributed practice, students review or revisit the information throughout the years, continuing to strengthen their neural networks. The transfer of information into long-term storage can take some students typically days and sometimes weeks.

Based on time needed for formation of synapses, information should be reviewed or processed 10 minutes after learning it, then 24 hours later, and then again 7 days later to ensure a solid foundation of the newly formed neural network (Jensen, 1998). As shown on the diagram below, more than 90 percent of information is forgotten within 24 hours. Reviewing information within 24 hours helps increase retention. After a week, retention goes back down but not as much as it did in the initial 24 hours. Notice that the degree of recall increases after each review session. Each time you review information, you help neural connections become stronger so more information can be retrieved and less forgotten. Of course, review shouldn't end after 7 days. Review should continue but longer intervals are acceptable.

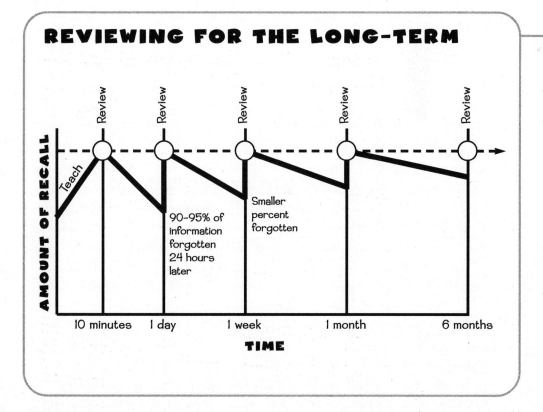

REVIEWING FOR THE LONG-TERM

AMOUNT OF RECALL

Teach

Review — Review — Review — Review — Review

90-95% of information forgotten 24 hours later

Smaller percent forgotten

10 minutes   1 day   1 week   1 month   6 months

TIME

Distributed practice over time increases the amount of recall of learning. One way new learning transfers from short-term to long-term memory is by reviewing the information 10 minutes after learning it, 24 hours (1 day) later, and then 7 days (1 week) later. Continue to review after that but at longer intervals.

SLEEP CONSOLIDATES LEARNING

It's ironic that some students stay up all night studying for a test, thinking that they will remember information better if they spend more time reviewing it. But in reality, the lack of sleep becomes a disservice.

During sleep the brain processes information that has been obtained that day. Research shows that the more a person learns during the day, the more dreaming, or REM (rapid eye movement), occurs at night. "REM sleep period assumes about 25 percent of our entire night's rest; and it is thought to be critical to memory" (Markowitz, 1999). Bruce McNaughton, Ph.D., from the University of Arizona, suggests that during sleep periods the hippocampus rehearses what it learned. "REM sleep is crucial for organizing pieces and the associations between them needed for forming lasting memories" (Ratey, 2001).

Emphasize to students how important sleep is to memory. Encourage them to get a full night's sleep before a test.

BEM PRINCIPLE AND THE POWER OF CLOSURES

Psychologists use the term "BEM Principle" to explain the order in which people are most likely to recall information (Beginning, End, and Middle). During a learning episode, students remember best the information they learned first, followed by the information they learned last. They least remember the information that comes in the middle. There are many other variables that affect retention of information (such as novelty, personal information, and highly emotional information), but understanding the BEM Principle can help you enhance your students' retention of information.

Research has verified that an easy way to remember something is to make it new and different. That's because the brain tends to pay more attention to something it has never encountered before. Students generally remember the first and last moments of a lesson because of novelty. The beginning of a lesson usually has a grabber (anticipatory set) that is novel. In the middle of a lesson, the novelty wears off and the mind starts to drift, so the information is not as easily remembered. At this time the brain is ready to think about (or process) what it just learned. The brain naturally needs this "settling time" to process or make meaning out of newly presented information. Toward the end of a lesson, the brain, which just experienced some settling time, is ready for something new again. The anticipation triggers excitement, which increases adrenaline flow, necessary for memory to occur. This in turn increases oxygen flow to the brain, enhancing attention.

The middle part of a lesson need not be a total waste, however. It is during this settling time that practicing is crucial. Students need to actively practice what they

IT'S A FACT!

Harvard Medical School researchers, led by assistant professor of psychiatry Robert Stickgold, found that people who went to sleep after learning information and practicing a new task remembered more about the information and task the next day than people who stayed up all night after learning the same thing. "We think getting that first night's sleep starts the process of memory consolidation," says Stickgold. "It seems that memories normally wash out of the brain unless some process nails them down."

just learned through guided practice and independent practice. The brain's settling time is about 10 to 20 minutes into the lesson (1 minute per age of the child, plus or minus 2; in other words, a 12-year-old's settling time starts about 12 minutes into the lesson). So a practice session should occur about 10 minutes after the new learning. For example, during a writing or math mini-lesson, use the first 10 minutes to teach a new strategy, then have students practice the strategy on their own for the next 3 to 10 minutes. (The amount of time depends on the learner's background, the complexity and novelty of information, as well as stress and learning styles.) But be sure to leave time for the *closure,* or ending.

With new information being taught at the beginning of a lesson and students practicing their learning in the middle, the closure is often left out due to lack of time. As we've established earlier, the ending is the second-most important learning time of a lesson and should not be left out. Rather, this is a great time for the students to solidify their neural networks with a review. The review must be done by the students, not the teacher. Here are some of my favorite closures:

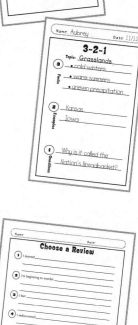

1 **DOOR PASS:** Photocopy "Door Pass" (page 20) for quick reviews at the end of a lesson before students leave. Distribute a Door Pass to each student and decide how you want students to review what they learned. They could write a summary, ask a question about something they still don't understand, write about how the topic relates to their life, or write down three facts that they learned.

2 **3-2-1:** In this activity, you or your students can create the criteria for review. For example, you can have students write three new facts that they learned, two questions that they have, and one sentence that uses their name and the concept to show that they understood what was taught. Photocopy the right half of page 20 for each student.

3 **CHOOSE A REVIEW:** You can use this activity all year long. Photocopy "Choose a Review" (page 21) for each person or copy it on the board or on poster paper. Have students choose one of the review statements and respond in writing. Students can even write their responses on the Door Pass.

4 **QUICK DRAW:** This activity is a perfect opportunity for the artists in your class to express themselves. Photocopy "Quick Draw" (page 22) for each student. Invite students to draw a picture of what they learned, the most important information, how they perceive a character looks, or anything else that shows they understood the topic.

5 **SIMILE SUMMARY:** Creating similes helps students see how a new concept relates to a more familiar concept. Photocopy "Simile Summary" (page 22) for each student. Challenge students to describe how a concept they just learned is similar to another concept, and explain why.

Name: _____   Date: _____

3-2-1

Topic: _____

③ _____
_____
_____

② _____
_____

① _____

Name: _____   Date: _____

Door Pass

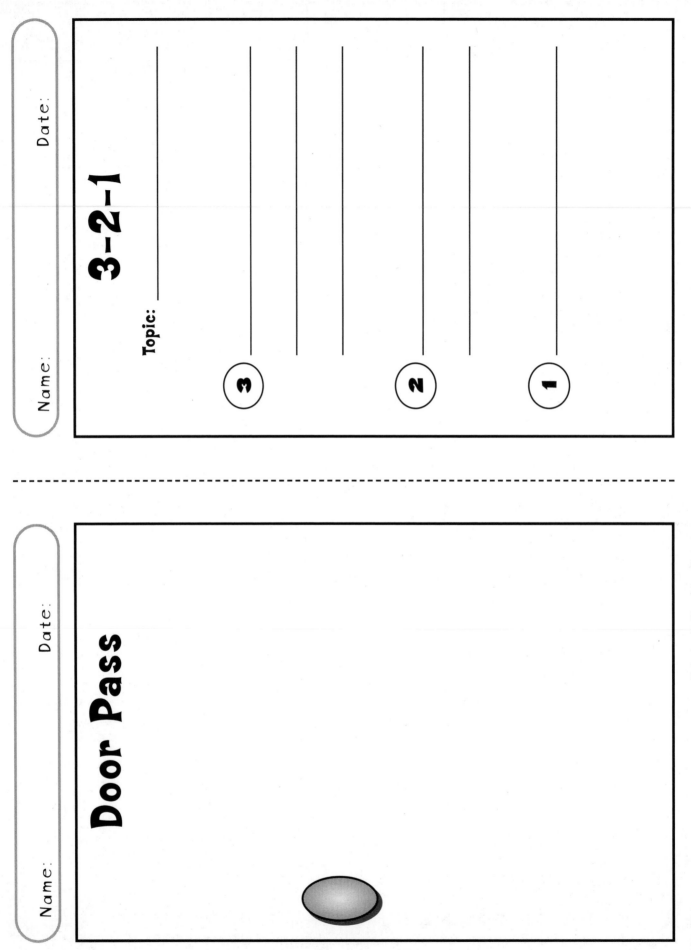

Choose a Review

1 I learned _____

_____

_____

2 I'm beginning to wonder _____

_____

_____

3 I feel _____

_____

_____

4 I rediscovered _____

_____

_____

5 The most important thing about _____

is _____

_____

6 I can relate to _____

because _____

_____

Quick Draw

Name: _____ Date: _____

Simile Summary

_____

is like a _____

because _____

_____

_____

CHAPTER 4

POWERFUL WAYS TO REVIEW

Even as you teach a new lesson, there are several techniques you can use to enhance the review process and make sure the information sticks in students' memories. In this chapter, we'll look at what current research says about how the brain learns and remembers information. Then we'll put research into practice, giving you ideas on how to enrich your lessons and review sessions. Finally, you'll find a more elaborate classroom activity that supports the research.

MOVEMENTS FOR MEMORY

RESEARCH SAYS...

The mind remembers information better when the whole body and emotions are involved. In a study done at Scripps College in Claremont, California, Dr. Kushner divided a group of people into three categories: those who engaged in low levels of exercise, those who engaged in high levels of exercise, and those who did not exercise at all. The researchers then spent three hours giving participants tests on memory, reasoning, and reaction time. They found that "exercisers scored significantly higher on working-memory tests, reasoning, and reaction time." In other words, increased blood flow to the brain due to exercise helps you remember better.

Dr. Max Vercruyssen of the University of Southern California discovered how the body's posture affects learning. He found that on average, standing increased heart rate by 10 extra beats per minute. That means more blood goes to the brain, increasing neural firing within the central nervous system. "Standing speeds up information processing 5 to 20 percent, compared to sitting down" (Jensen, 1996).

> **"**Movement is the door to learning.**"**
>
> —PAUL DENNISON

FROM RESEARCH TO PRACTICE

◉ Rather than have students draw graphs on paper, invite them to form 3-D graphs with their bodies. For example, students can form a circle graph and use string to divide students with pets from those who have no pets.

◉ Engage students in role-playing, debates, and simulations to enhance learning. Encourage students to dramatize a battle from a particular war or act out how a literary character might be feeling.

◉ Frequent breaks give students' minds time to process new information. During a break the brain gets time off from focusing on what the teacher is saying, and instead can give it meaning. Breaks that involve movement or exercise allow more blood to flow to the brain and promote optimal learning. Exercises could include toe touches; arm crossovers (make an X with outstretched arms, switching which arm goes on top); neck circles; jumping jacks; arms in air (stretch one arm straight into air and bend at waist in same direction, then switch arms); and running in place. Since the left side of the brain controls the right side of the body and vice versa, these cross-lateral exercises help both sides of the brain communicate with each other better (Dennison, 1992).

◉ Offer several stand-up breaks between and during lessons. Have students switch desks and go to a different part of the room. Even a quick stretch break is very effective. It allows more oxygen to the brain, fueling it to be more alert and active.

◉ Create an action or movement to help students recall an important concept. For example, to help my students remember what a noun is, I have them point to objects in the room as they recite: "A *noun* is a person (point to a person), place (point to a place), thing (point to a thing), and idea (hold palm face up, flat in air)." Every time I mention the word *verb*, students run in place. An adjective "describes" so I have my students raise their hands in the air and run them down their bodies (not touching), as if they are describing themselves with their hands. They never forget these parts of speech.

◉ Give students opportunities to show that they're learning during each lesson. This can be done very creatively and actively. For example, students can display "thumbs up" if the statement is a fact; "thumbs down" if the statement is an opinion. They can also clap their hands, stand up and sit down, or jump in response to cues.

EXTENSION: SUPER SLEUTH REVIEW

Objective Students walk around the classroom to find fellow classmates who can answer review questions. Then they write down three new ideas or facts that they learned from other students during this review session.

Grouping Whole class, but provide each student with his or her own copy of Super Sleuth Review

To Do

1 Make a copy of Super Sleuth Review (page 34). In each square, write a question pertaining to a lesson or unit that you want to review with the class. You can fill in all of the squares or leave a few blank for students to create their own review questions. At right is an example of questions that I created the day before a test on the unit of the brain.

2 When you have finished writing your questions, make a photocopy of the filled-in sheet for each student.

3 Distribute copies to students. Together, read the directions at the top of the page to make sure students understand what to do. If you left some boxes blank, give students enough time to write their own review questions.

4 Tell students that you'll be walking around to listen to their quality conversations and to learn from them as well. This will help students stay on task better. Feel free to answer some questions, too. Students will be lining up next to you!

5 Depending on the kinds of questions posed, give students 15 to 30 minutes to circulate and get answers from classmates. (Higher-level questions may take more time to answer.)

6 When everyone has finished and returned to their desk, have them turn over their sheets and write down three new ideas or facts that they learned from classmates. If they can't think of anything, encourage them to write down information that was reinforced for them.

7 Encourage students to take their sheets home to use for review.

Super Sleuth Review

Name: _____

Topic: **The Brain**

Directions: Walk around the classroom and find someone to answer one of the questions below. When a student answers a question, have him or her initial that question box. Each student may sign only one box. The goal is to learn from different students' responses. If you don't understand someone's answer, ask him or her to explain further. When time is up, write three new ideas or facts that you learned from other students on the back of this sheet.

List 3 of the 8 different multiple intelligences. Initials: _____	What is the difference between the brain and the mind? Initials: _____	Tell your favorite, amazing fact that you learned from this unit. Initials: _____	What part of the brain is considered the "seat of emotion" and what is its role in learning? Initials: _____
Explain why the cerebellum is so important to learning. Initials: _____	How do neurons communicate? Initials: _____	Explain if you are more right or left brain dominant and why. Initials: _____	What are some things that you can do to enhance the memory of facts? Initials: _____
What are some things that you can do to enrich your brain? Initials: _____	Initials: _____	Initials: _____	Initials: _____

Memorizing Strategies & Other Brain-Based Activities Page 34 Scholastic Teaching Resources

KNOW YOUR MNEMONICS

RESEARCH SAYS...

Mnemonics, which means "assisting the memory," is a technique that allows learners to remember information using short retrieval cues. The idea is to break down information so that the brain can recall the big picture in smaller chunks. Some mnemonics rhyme, such as:

◎ *Columbus sailed the ocean blue in fourteen hundred ninety-two.*

◎ *The number you are dividing by, turn upside down and multiply.* (This is a rule for dividing by fractions.)

Other types of mnemonics reduce a large body of information by using only the first letters for retrieval. For example:

◎ **M**y **V**ery **E**arnest **M**other **J**ust **S**erved **U**s **N**ine **P**izzas (the planets of the solar system, in order of their proximity to the sun: Mercury, Venus, Earth, Mars, Jupiter, Saturn, Uranus, Neptune, Pluto)

◎ CANU (the four states that meet at one corner: Colorado, Arizona, New Mexico, Utah)

What Works: Research About Teaching and Learning, a study conducted by the U.S. Department of Education (1986), concluded that "mnemonics help students remember more information faster and retain it longer." The key is to introduce and apply mnemonics early in the learning stage and use them frequently. Eventually, the mnemonic and its corresponding information will be very easy for students to recall.

FROM RESEARCH TO PRACTICE

Here are some popular mnemonics you can introduce to students:

◎ *Lefty loosy, righty tighty* (how to turn knobs and screws)

◎ *ROY G. BIV* (rainbow color spectrum: red, orange, yellow, green, blue, indigo, violet)

◎ *Every **G**ood **B**oy **D**oes **F**ine* (line notes on the treble clef)

◎ *Thirty days hath September, April, June and November; when short February is done, all the rest have 31* (number of days in each month)

◎ *Bless **M**y **D**ear **A**unt **S**ally* (order of operations in an algebraic equation: brackets, multiplication, division, addition, subtraction)

◎ *"i" before "e" except after "c"* (spelling)

◎ *Bad grammar will mar a report* (spelling)

◎ *He screamed "eee" as he passed by the cemetery* (spelling)

◎ *The principal is my pal* (spelling)

◉ To remember states and their capitals, identify sound-alike words and link them with visual imagery. For example, students can picture a group of boys hoeing a potato patch to remember Boise, Idaho. See *Yo, Sacramento!* by Will Cleveland and Mark Alvarez (Millbrook Press, 1997) for more tips on remembering states and capitals.

◉ For tips on how to remember the names of U.S. Presidents, see *Yo, Millard Fillmore!* by Will Cleveland and Mark Alvarez (Millbrook Press, 1997).

EXTENSION: VOCABU-TOONS

Objective Students use the *keyword method*, a mnemonic system to help remember vocabulary words. They construct a visual image that connects a vocabulary word with a familiar, concrete rhyming word that shares a common feature.

Grouping Partners

To Do

1 Show students samples of vocabulary cartoons—sketches that illustrate and help you remember vocabulary words. You may want to create your own or use examples from the book *Vocabulary Cartoons* by Sam, Max, and Bryan Burchers (New Monic Books, 1997). (See right.)

2 Photocopy and distribute "Vocabu-Toons" (page 35) to each student pair. Partner students and have each pair design a Vocabu-Toon using assigned vocabulary words.

3 After students have finished creating their own Vocabu-Toon, encourage each pair to present their cartoon and the vocabulary word it teaches to the whole class. Consider photocopying and compiling each pair's Vocabu-Toon into a book for every student to take home and review.

> **TIP**
>
> Vocabulary researchers Baumann and Kameenui (1991) found that the *keyword method*, a mnemonic technique, is one of the most effective methods for remembering vocabulary words.

WADDLE
(WAH dle)
to walk with short steps swaying from side to side

Sounds like: **BOTTLE**

"Babies with **BOTTLES WADDLE**."

❑ Ducks always **WADDLE** when they walk.
❑ Sailors on ships **WADDLE**.
❑ Larry **WADDLED** from the dinner table after eating his third helping of apple pie.

SUMMARIZING SUCCESS

RESEARCH SAYS...

Summarizing is a form of repetition and processing, a way to assess students' understanding of the lesson. When students summarize, they review the information they learned and explain it in their own words. When they put information in their own words, they retrieve prior knowledge from their long-term memory to help make sense of the summary. Thus they connect new learning to prior knowledge and give meaning to the information so that it can also stay in long-term memory (Sousa, 2001).

Students need to be active summarizers in order to attach meaning to the learning. At the end of a lesson (during closure), encourage students to actively summarize the topic in their own words by showing, writing, or talking about what they learned. Students should also summarize information after reading a section from a book so that they don't get too far into the story without having a clear idea of what's going on. Marzano, Pickering, and Pollock (2001) made the following generalizations about summarizing a reading passage:

1. Students must "delete some information, substitute some information, and keep some information."
2. To do those actions, students must analyze the reading information on a deep level.
3. Students are better able to summarize when they understand the "explicit structure" of the reading passage. When students are aware of the structure, they can attend to the most important sections of the passage. Knowing where the most important information is located aids in creating a summary.

FROM RESEARCH TO PRACTICE

◎ Show students how they can use their hand as a helpful visual for summarizing a story. Each finger and the palm of the hand represent one of these questions: who, what, where, when, why, and how.

◎ Teach students these four steps to a great summary:
1. Preview, read, and review the selection.
2. Identify the main points (for example, *This section is about... and the point is...*).
3. Draw a visual (such as a map, web, chart, Venn diagram, or herringbone) to organize information.
4. Restate/paraphrase (for example, ask when, where, what to do, and meaning what?)

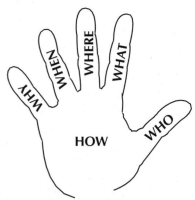

EXTENSION: MIND MAPPING

Objective

Students practice *mind mapping*, a brain-compatible technique that enhances depth of learning, understanding, and application of content. According to Mel Levine (2002), mind mapping is a great review tool because "the best way to remember something is to change it, to transform the information in some manner. If it's visual, make it verbal; if it's verbal, create a diagram or picture of it." By creating mind maps of notes taken from class, students will learn it better, remember it better, and make the information more meaningful.

Grouping

Partners (When students feel more comfortable with mind mapping, encourage them to work on their own. Mind mapping is ideal for individuals because students organize information based on how they comprehend and connect the ideas.)

Materials

◎ Unlined paper
◎ Colored pencils or markers

To Do

1 Explain to students that a mind map is a pictorial or symbolic representation of concepts that are linked together. It is a brain-compatible technique that may be used for note taking, presentations, assessments, or any other function that requires memorization, transition, retention, or association of ideas and concepts.

2 Photocopy "Mind Mapping Guidelines" on page 30 onto a transparency. Go through each guideline with students, modeling each step on chart paper so students understand what a mind map looks like. (See page 36 for an example of a mind map.)

3 Continue to model mind mapping with different reading passages until students understand the concept. While you're modeling, ask students to follow along on their own paper.

4 Explain that in a completed mind map the focus is on the topic's big ideas, not the details. These bigger extensions help students write a summary since the information is organized. Show students what information needs to be kept, discarded, and substituted.

MIND MAPPING GUIDELINES

1. Represent the main topic (pictorially or symbolically) at the center of the paper.

2. Represent related topics in spokes around the main topic.

3. Use COLOR. The more colorful or unique the representation, the more likely your brain will remember it.

4. Use only key words or phrases and PRINT them. The brain recognizes and remembers the printed word more readily than words written in cursive.

5. Represent ideas with symbols. This personalizes the concept at the same time you translate it into a concrete representation.

6. Use arrows or underlines to highlight the important ideas.

7. Cluster or group similar facts related to the main topic.

 Photocopy and distribute the "Mind Map Summary" to students to show how to turn a mind map into a written summary.

 Distribute paper (preferably unlined) and colored pencils or markers to students. Provide students with topics to mind-map.

QUALITY QUESTIONS

RESEARCH SAYS...

Questioning sessions emphasize important pieces of information. The brain automatically focuses on the most important information when a question is asked. Researchers found that when a person is asked a question requiring a yes or no answer, an amazing thing happens: "After the answer has been given, our brain continues, unconsciously, to process alternatives to the answer." Questions generate sustained, enriching brain activity (Jensen, 1996).

According to research, the higher the quality of questions asked, the more the brain is challenged to think. Researchers found that learner performance scores improved when the questions asked of learners increased in depth (Jensen, 1995). Bloom's Taxonomy categorizes types of questions according to their complexity. Higher-level-thinking questions fall into the following categories: evaluation, synthesis, and analysis. This is not to say that the other three levels—knowledge, comprehension, and application—are not important. All levels of questioning are important, but those that challenge the mind are even more so.

FROM RESEARCH TO PRACTICE

◎ Practice tests and reviews help students focus on the most important concepts in a unit lesson. I usually ask students questions about the topic periodically throughout the day. See Chapter 5 (beginning on page 39) for a variety of review games students can play.

◎ After reading a selection, have students generate two lists of questions:
  1. **unleaded (recall or closed) questions**, which can be answered by a word or short phrase; and
  2. **leaded (open-ended) questions**, which require more critical thinking and higher-level thinking.

Challenge students to write about four or five questions of each kind, then have them exchange papers with a partner and answer their partner's questions. To help students ask more higher-level questions, copy "Bloom's Taxonomy Question Starters" (page 37) on a transparency and display on the overhead.

EXTENSION: QUESTION SPINNER

Objective   Students will use a spinner to answer comprehension questions after reading a chosen selection. This activity helps students stay focused during the reading and enhances comprehension. Higher-level thinking is going on in the brain as students respond to each spinner question.

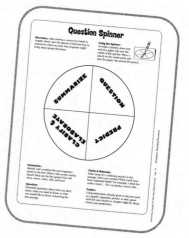

 Grouping   3 or 4 students

Materials   ◎ Question Spinner (page 38)
                 ◎ Reading selection (from a content area or narrative book)

 To Do

1 Divide the class into groups of three or four students.

2 Students in each group take turns reading parts of the selection. After a student has read a section, have her spin the spinner to see what kind of reading response is required. For example, if the spinner lands on "Summarize," the student summarizes what she just read.

3 The next student takes a turn by reading the following section and spins. Again, she responds to the section according to where the spinner lands.

4 Continue until the whole reading section is completed.

SOCIALIZATION SOLUTIONS

RESEARCH SAYS...

he brain is a social brain (Gazzaniga, 1985). Humans become what they are through their interactions with others and the environment. According to research done by Johnson and Johnson (1999), there are five defining elements of cooperative learning:

1. **positive interdependence** (sink or swim together)
2. **face-to-face interaction** (encouraging and celebrating success)
3. **individual and group accountability** (each student has goals to meet for group success)
4. **interpersonal and small-group skills** (leadership, trust, conflict resolution)
5. **group processing** (evaluating groups' functioning)

According to research, retention increases 90 to 95 percent when students teach one another (Sousa, 2001). That's because the presenter needs to know the information very well in order to explain it. This gives students the opportunity to evaluate and synthesize the material.

FROM RESEARCH TO PRACTICE

◎ Break down a unit of study into subtopics and assign each group of students a subtopic in which they can become experts. Then invite each group to share or teach the information to the whole class. For example, I might take a chapter from a social studies book and have two students specialize in a subtopic. After they have become thoroughly familiar with their subtopic, they must teach their section to other students using visuals, personal examples (if applicable), transparencies, and so on. I encourage students to get creative with their presentation: put on a newscast, perform a puppet play, create a skit, conduct an interview, and so on. Other students take notes as each group presents its information.

◎ Think–pair–share is a cooperative learning experience in which students think about a concept that the teacher provides, pair up with someone, and share what they think about the concept with a partner. (See page 51 for a variation on this activity.)

EXTENSION: GROUP ACTIVITY EVALUATION

Objective Students will help create a rubric to evaluate group performance after a cooperative learning game or activity. Creating a group activity rubric is a great segue into the next chapter on review games. By reviewing the criteria for cooperative learning and evaluating themselves after a game, students become more aware of the kind of social skills necessary to successfully review content in a game format.

Grouping Whole class

To Do

1 Read aloud the book *It Takes a Village* by Jane Cowen-Fletcher (Scholastic, 1994). This book stresses that it takes a group of people to help individuals become the best they can be. The environment plays a major role in what people become.

2 Engage students in a discussion about the book and what they thought about it. Ask: Who makes up your "village"? (*Families, friends, teachers, classmates, and so on*) Do you think our classroom is a village? (*Yes*) How? (*People help each other, share with each other, encourage each other.*)

3 As a class, discuss what a group activity should look and sound like as well as what it should NOT look and sound like. Draw the T-chart at right on the board and fill it in with the class.

Classroom Group Activity

Looks and sounds like:	Does NOT look and sound like:

4 Based on the chart, create a rubric with students that evaluates every group activity. On butcher paper, write the title "Group Activity Evaluation" and list the categories (i.e., types of group behavior) that will be evaluated. Include a scoring system like the one below:

OUTSTANDING	MEDIOCRE	NEEDS IMPROVEMENT
3 points	2 points	1 point

5 Post the chart and keep it up year-round so that students can rate themselves and their group after a group activity. (See the "Game Rubric" on page 42 for an example.)

Super Sleuth Review

Name:

Topic:

Directions: Walk around the classroom and find someone to answer one of the questions below. When a student answers a question, have him or her initial that question box. Each student may sign only one box. The goal is to learn from different students' responses. If you don't understand someone's answer, ask him or her to explain further. When time is up, write three new ideas or facts that you learned from other students on the back of this sheet.

Initials: ———	Initials: ———	Initials: ———
Initials: ———	Initials: ———	Initials: ———
Initials: ———	Initials: ———	Initials: ———

Vocabu-Toons

Vocabulary Word: _____

Pronunciation: _____

Definition and part of speech: _____

_____

Sounds like (rhyming word): _____

Directions: Create a sentence with the vocabulary word and a rhyming word that makes it easy to remember. Draw a picture below to illustrate the sentence.

On the back of this page, write three sentences using the vocabulary word:

1. Use the vocabulary word in a way that is relevant to you and your life.

2. Transform the vocabulary word by adding prefixes or suffixes. For example, *commuter = commuting*

3. Use the vocabulary word any way you like.

MIND MAP:
Tender Lovin' Care of the Brain

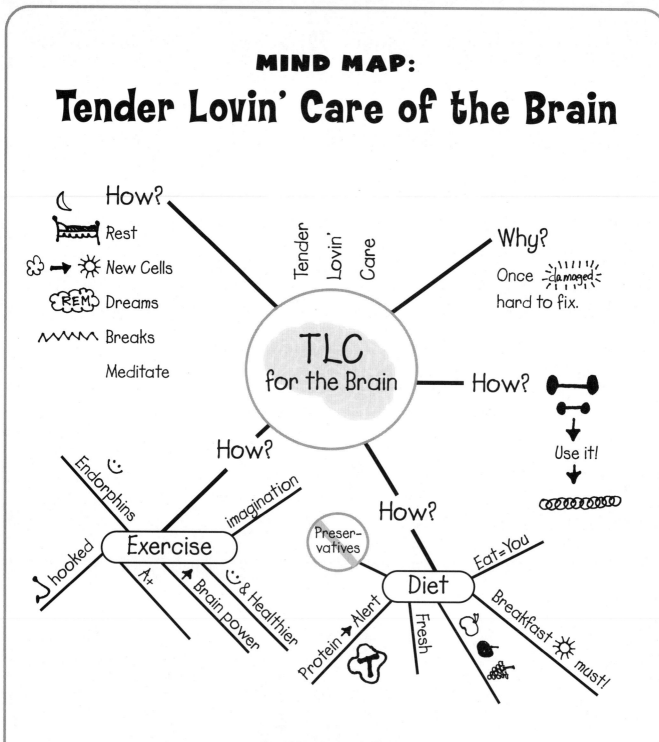

Tender Lovin' Care

TLC for the Brain

How?
- Rest
- New Cells
- Dreams
- Breaks
- Meditate

Why?
Once damaged hard to fix.

How?
Use it!

How?
Exercise
- Endorphins
- hooked
- A+
- imagination
- Brain power
- & Healthier

How?
Diet
- Preservatives
- Protein → Alert
- Fresh
- Eat=You
- Breakfast a must!

SUMMARY:

There are many ways to provide tender lovin' care for the brain. Eating a healthy diet with lots of fresh fruits and vegetables makes the brain healthier and more alert. Exercising encourages endorphins to flow through the entire brain, encouraging brain activity. The more exercise we do, the more oxygen reaches the brain, giving it more brainpower. Finally, the brain needs a good night's sleep to rejuvenate cells and consolidate the day's learning. These are just a few ways to give the brain some TLC.

Bloom's Taxonomy Question Starters

Knowledge

Who, what, where, when…?

How would you explain…?

Which one…?

Can you list…?

Can you select…?

Comprehension

How would you classify…?

How would you rephrase…?

How would you compare/contrast…?

What is the main idea…?

Which statements support…?

What facts or ideas show…?

Application

What would result if…?

What other way could you…?

How would you organize…?

How would you use…?

How would you solve…?

How would you apply…?

What approach would you use to…?

Analysis

What are the parts or features of…?

How would you categorize…?

What evidence can you find…?

What is the relationship between…?

How would you classify…?

What motive is behind…?

What is the theme of…?

Synthesis

Suppose you could ____, what would you do?

What changes would you make to solve…?

What would happen if…?

How would you adapt ____ to make it different?

What could be done to maximize/minimize…?

What could be combined to create…?

Can you think of an original way to…?

Can you formulate a theory for…?

Evaluation

Do you agree with the actions…?

What is your opinion of…?

Would it be better if…?

How would you evaluate…?

What would you select…?

What judgment would you make about…?

What information would you use to support the view…?

How would you prioritize the facts…?

How would you compare the characters…?

Question Spinner

Directions: After reading a section of a book or chapter aloud, spin the spinner to find out how to respond to what you read. Your response might bring about group discussion.

Using the Spinner:
To make a pointer, place one end of a paper clip over the center of the spinner. Place a pencil on the center point and spin the paper clip around the pencil.

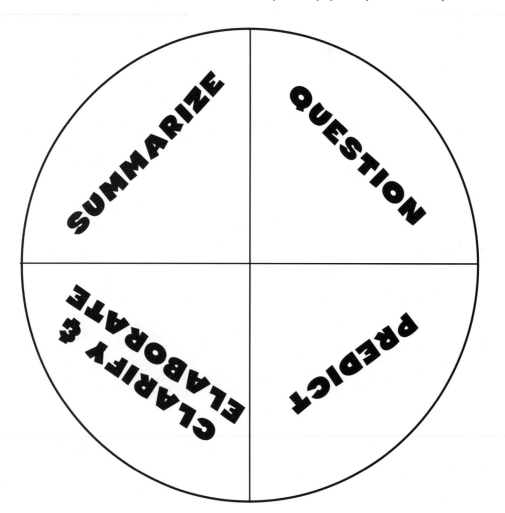

Summarize:
Identify and condense the most important points in the text. What is this section mainly about? What are the key points? Who did what, where, when, why, and how?

Question:
Formulate questions about what you don't know, what you need to know, or what you would like to know concerning the text passage.

Clarify & Elaborate:
Make sense of a confusing section in the passage. What was unclear? What could have been explained better? For example, *I think the author meant… This vocabulary word is like…*

Predict:
Using information already given in the text (such as a graphic organizer, picture, or text), guess what the next section or chapter might be about. Check your predictions.

CHAPTER 5

REVIEW GAMES

> "A laugh a day keeps the blah bug away!"
>
> —KAREN LOOMANS

What better way to review key facts and general information than by playing fun and engaging games? You'll be surprised at how students become much more motivated to learn information when they know that they'll be called upon to show off their knowledge in fun-filled games. In addition, playing games encourages social interaction among students, giving them a chance to hone their social skills. And, as students play review games that reinforce concepts they've learned, their neural networks are strengthened and the information has an increasingly better chance of making it to long-term memory.

The 10 games in this section offer students a variety of ways to review accumulated information throughout a learning unit. They fit with any content area, such as social studies, science, math, or grammar. All you have to do is supply the content you want to review in each game. Play any of these games about one or two days before a unit test.

10 SUPER-FUN REVIEW GAMES

1. Dynamic Dominoes
2. Trio Tournament
3. Think–Pair–Check
4. Looping Game
5. Grab-a-Slate
6. You're It!
7. Battle Bus
8. Dice-a-Rama
9. Plus/Minus Game
10. Create-a-Game

> " Laughter is the shortest distance between two people. "
>
> —Victor Borge

For each game, you'll find:

◉ **For Teachers page** — includes a quick overview of the game, a list of materials you'll need, plus how to get ready to play the game

◉ **Game Plan page** — provides students with easy, step-by-step directions on how to play the game

◉ **Reproducible question cards, tally sheets, and/or game sheets**

MANAGEMENT TIPS

1 You may want to designate a Game Day each week, when you'll play a game to review a lesson or unit. Let students know when Game Day is and what information will be covered. Sometimes I even let my students know the questions that I'll be asking. I want them to do well and feel successful. For study tips, give each student a copy of "25 Study Secrets for Students" (page 77).

2 On the For Teachers pages, I suggest a group size that worked well for my class. You may want to look at your classroom needs and adjust the group size accordingly.

In grouping students together, you may choose to put higher-ability students with lower-ability students to encourage peer-teaching relationships. Or you may want to challenge your gifted/talented students and put them together in a group. You may decide to play some games with your lower-ability students so that you can emphasize certain review questions. Of course, you may also want to let students choose their own groups. Choice is a great motivator. However, make sure nobody gets left out.

3 For most games, we provide a reproducible sheet of blank cards on which you can write review questions. Decide how many questions you'd like to review to determine how many copies of the reproducible cards you'll need to make.

I used a question-and-answer format in creating the sample game cards, but there are several other formats you can use to review information. Here are some suggestions:

> question–answer
> word–definition
> word–explanation
> word–example
> word–picture
> word–related part (or whole–part)

synonym–antonym (or synonym–synonym)

math problem–solution or answer

statement–fact or opinion

statement–complete sentence, run-on, or fragment

 If possible, copy the Game Plan for students on a blank transparency sheet and display it on an overhead projector. This way, all students can easily view the directions while they play the game.

 You'll notice that there are blank lines at the bottom of the Game Plan sheets. Fill them in to let students know where to return the games when they're finished and what to do while they wait for the rest of the class to finish—it's great for classroom management!

 At the end of each game, have students fill out a Game Rubric (page 42) to evaluate their group. This way, all members are held accountable for the group's performance and there's less chance of one player running the show. (If you wish, you can create your own rubric based on your expectations for cooperative learning.)

Give each student a copy of "Using the Game Rubric" (page 43) and discuss each point with the class so students fully understand what's expected of them. You may also want to make a transparency of the sheet and display it on the overhead at the end of each game to remind students what each section of the rubric means.

Have fun! Remember: Emotion embedded into content makes for a VERY powerful memory lane!

Game Rubric

Group Members: _____

_____

TASK	OUTSTANDING	YES	ALMOST	NO
1. My group completed the game fairly. Explain: _____ _____	4	3	2	1
2. I participated equally and encouraged my group members to participate, too. Explain: _____ _____	4	3	2	1
3. My group stayed on task and got along well. Explain: _____ _____	4	3	2	1
4. I did my part in studying for this review game. Explain: _____ _____	4	3	2	1
TOTAL SCORE				

5. I admire_____

because he/she _____

6. I want to remember the following information better: _____

_____

_____

Using the Game Rubric

The game rubric is designed to help you understand what is expected from you while playing a game. Every person in your group should fill in a rubric at the end of a game. Here is an explanation of each criterion:

Use these numbers to evaluate how well you and your group met each criterion:

4 – Outstanding: We went above and beyond!

3 – Yes: We did a good job.

2 – Almost: We could have done better.

1 – No: We didn't do well at all.

1. **My group completed the game fairly.**
Did your group accomplish the goal of the game? Why or why not? Were there any problems that kept you from completing the game? What were they?

2. **I participated equally and encouraged my group to participate, too.**
Did everyone in the group contribute equally to the game? If someone held back and did not help out much, then that person did not participate equally. If one student took over, then that person did not participate equally, either. Did you encourage other players to get involved? Explain why you rated yourself the way you did.

3. **My group stayed on task and got along well.**
Did everyone in your group work cooperatively? Show a positive attitude? Study for the review? Encourage and praise other players? Explain why or why not.

4. **I did my part in studying for this review game.**
Were you prepared for this game? Did you contribute to your group? Did you need to study more? Explain why or why not.

5. **I admire _____ because he/she...**
Did someone in your group stand out more than others? Here's an opportunity to praise a fellow teammate for his or her contributions.

6. **I want to remember the following information better:**
What questions did you miss during the game? What concepts do you need to study before the test/quiz?

Dynamic Dominoes

Overview

Invite students to play this self-checking version of dominoes, in which they match the question side of a domino with the answer side of another. When completed correctly, the dominoes will form a rectangle or circle.

Example: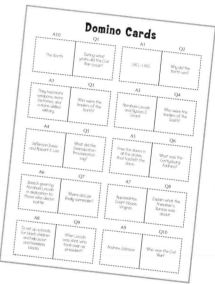

Q=Question
A=Answer

Suggested Grouping:

3 or 4 players

You'll Need:

◎ Domino Cards (page 46)

◎ Resealable plastic bags (one per group)

◎ Game Rubric (page 42)

◎ Game Plan (page 45)

Before Playing

1. Photocopy the Domino Cards sheet. (If you want more than 10 questions, make as many copies of the page as you need.) Decide on the topic you want students to review and write related questions and answers on the Domino Cards as follows:

   ◎ Write the first question in block Q1 and the answer in block A1.

   ◎ Write the second question in Q2 and its answer in A2.

   ◎ Continue until you reach the last question–answer set. (Notice that Q10 and A10 are not next to each other. By writing questions and answers in this format, you ensure a complete rectangle or circle.)

   ◎ To add more questions, make another copy of the Domino Cards sheet and make A10 the first block on the second page.

2. Photocopy one set of the completed Domino Cards for each group. Cut the dominoes apart along the dashed lines. Place one set of cut cards in a plastic bag for each group and distribute the bags.

3. Read and discuss the Game Plan with the class to make sure everyone understands how to play the game.

FOR STUDENTS

Dynamic Dominoes
Game Plan

Objective
To match the question side of each domino with the correct answer side.

How to Play

1. Assign a Materials Manager from your group to get the following items from your teacher:

  ◎ bag of Domino Cards

  ◎ Game Rubrics (one for each group member)

2. Spread the Domino Cards on a flat surface so that everyone in the group can see and reach the cards.

3. Work with your group to match the question on one domino to the correct answer on another domino. For example:

George Washington	Who was the 16th President?	Abraham Lincoln	Who created the New Deal Plan?

4. When you have correctly matched all the questions and answers, the Domino Cards should form a closed rectangle or circle.

5. After your group has finished playing the game, have each member fill in a Game Rubric to evaluate the group's performance. The Materials Manager should return the bag of cards and rubrics to _____.

6. Work on the following activity while you wait for all the other groups to finish playing:

_____

_____

Domino Cards

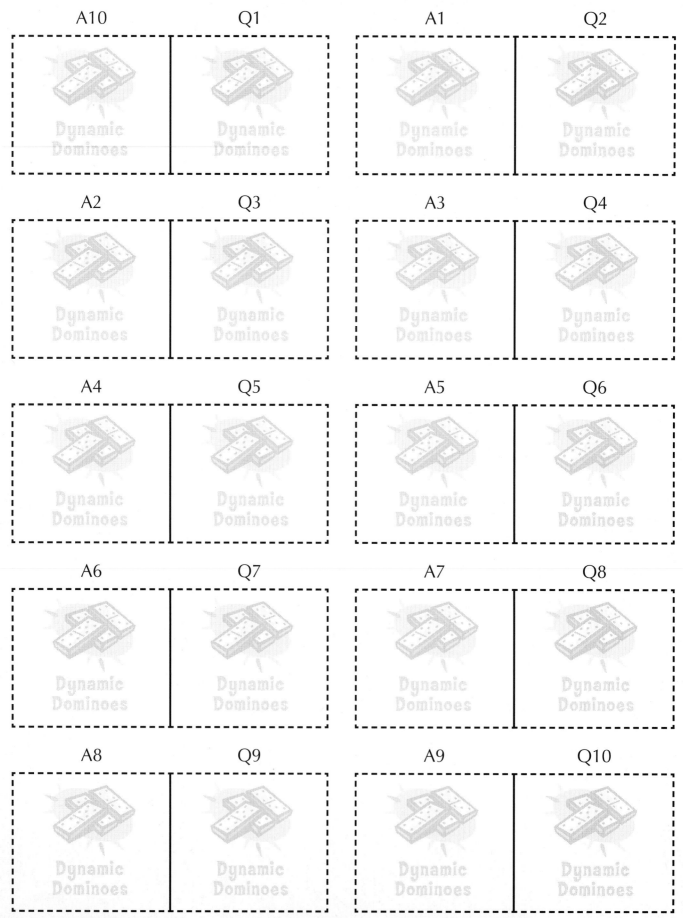

A10   Q1   A1   Q2

A2   Q3   A3   Q4

A4   Q5   A5   Q6

A6   Q7   A7   Q8

A8   Q9   A9   Q10

For Teachers

Trio Tournament

Overview

Challenge students to work cooperatively in groups of three to get the most correct answers in a series of 30 questions. The group with the most points is the winner.

Before Playing

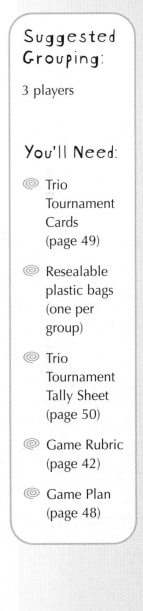

Suggested Grouping:

3 players

You'll Need:

- Trio Tournament Cards (page 49)
- Resealable plastic bags (one per group)
- Trio Tournament Tally Sheet (page 50)
- Game Rubric (page 42)
- Game Plan (page 48)

1. Make two copies of the Trio Tournament Cards page for a total of 30 question cards. Decide on the topic you want to review and write related questions on each card. Then turn over each page and write the answers directly behind the corresponding questions.

2. Make double-sided copies of the completed Trio Tournament Cards, making sure the answers on the back of each page match the questions in front. Cut the cards apart along the dashed lines. Place one set of 30 cards in a plastic bag for each group.

3. Divide the class into groups of three. Each person in the group will have a rotating role of Quizzer, Responder, or Recorder. (If you have one extra student, have him or her join one of the groups and share a role with another person in the group. If two students are left over, pair them up and combine the roles of Quizzer and Recorder.)

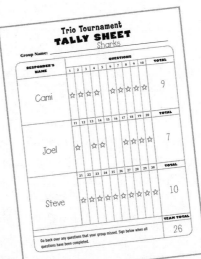

4. Distribute the bags along with a copy of the Trio Tournament Tally Sheet to each group.

5. Read and discuss the Game Plan with the class to make sure everyone understands how to play the game.

Trio Tournament
Game Plan

Objective
To answer correctly as many questions as possible in the role of Responder. The group with the most points wins.

How to Play

1. Assign a Materials Manager from your group to get the following items from your teacher:

- ◎ bag of Trio Tournament Cards
- ◎ Trio Tournament Tally Sheet
- ◎ Game Rubrics (one for each group member)

2. Select a name for your Trio Team and write it on the Trio Tournament Tally Sheet.

3. Assign each group member one of the following roles for the first round. (Members rotate roles after each round of 10 questions.)

- ◎ **Quizzer:** reads question cards aloud to the Responder
- ◎ **Responder:** answers the questions
- ◎ **Recorder:** marks correct or incorrect answers on the tally sheet (see step 4 below)

4. For each round, the Quizzer asks the Responder a set of 10 questions. If the Responder answers correctly, the Recorder draws a star on the space below the question number next to the Responder's name. If the answer is incorrect, leave the space blank.

5. Repeat step 4 for two more rounds, making sure group members rotate roles after each round. Each member should have played all three roles at the end of three rounds.

6. After three rounds, the last Recorder counts the number of correct answers and writes it on the tally sheet.

7. After your group has finished playing the game, have each member fill in a Game Rubric to evaluate the group's performance. The Materials Manager should return the bag of cards, the tally sheet, and rubrics to _____.

8. Work on the following activity while you wait for all the other groups to finish playing:

_____

Trio Tournament Cards

Trio Tournament
TALLY SHEET

Group Name: _____

RESPONDER'S NAME	QUESTIONS										TOTAL
	1	2	3	4	5	6	7	8	9	10	TOTAL
	11	12	13	14	15	16	17	18	19	20	TOTAL
	21	22	23	24	25	26	27	28	29	30	TOTAL
											TEAM TOTAL

Go back over any questions that your group missed. Sign below when all questions have been completed.

Think-Pair-Check

Overview

Pair up students to answer a series of 10 questions, five questions per partner. Partners then check each other's answers and help explain why an answer may be wrong.

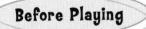

Before Playing

1. Photocopy the Think–Pair–Check Question Sheet. Write 10 questions for each pair of students to solve together. You can also divide the question sheet in half if you prefer each partner to answer five questions on his or her own.

2. Photocopy the completed Think–Pair–Check Question Sheet and the Think–Pair–Check Answer Sheet for each pair of students.

3. Pair up students. (I recommend partnering a higher-level student with a lower-level one.) If you have one extra student, you could pair up with the student or have him or her share the role with another student. Distribute the question and answer sheets to each pair.

4. Read and discuss the Game Plan with the class to make sure everyone understands how to do this activity.

Suggested Grouping:

2 players

You'll Need:

- Think–Pair–Check Question Sheet (page 53)
- Think–Pair–Check Answer Sheet (page 54)
- Pencil
- Answer key (provided by teacher)
- Game Rubric (page 42)
- Game Plan (page 52)

Think-Pair-Check
Game Plan

Objective
Each student in a pair answers five review questions. Partners check each other's answers. If any questions were answered incorrectly, the checking partner helps by explaining how to get the correct answer.

How to Play

1. Sit next to your partner so that Partner A sits on the "A" side of the paper and Partner B sits on the "B" side.

2. Write the answers to your set of five questions on your side of the answer sheet. When you and your partner are both finished, switch seats to check your partner's answers.

3. If an answer is correct, put a star next to the check box. If incorrect, leave the box blank to indicate that your partner needs to redo that answer.

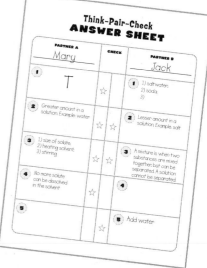

4. When you have finished checking each other's answers, switch seats again so that you can correct any wrong answers. If your partner missed a question because he or she didn't understand the concept, explain it to him or her.

5. Complete a Game Rubric to evaluate how you and your partner worked together. Then staple both your rubrics to the Think–Pair–Check Answer Sheet and place them

_____

6. Work on the following activity while you wait for all the other groups to finish playing:

_____

_____

Think-Pair-Check
QUESTION SHEET

(Write answers on the answer sheet.)

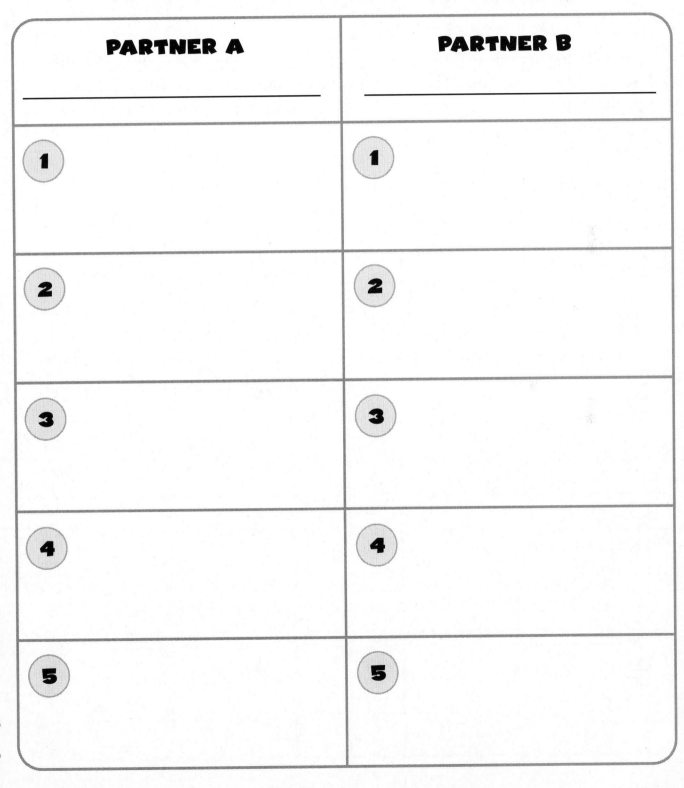

PARTNER A	PARTNER B
_____	_____
1	**1**
2	**2**
3	**3**
4	**4**
5	**5**

Think-Pair-Check
ANSWER SHEET

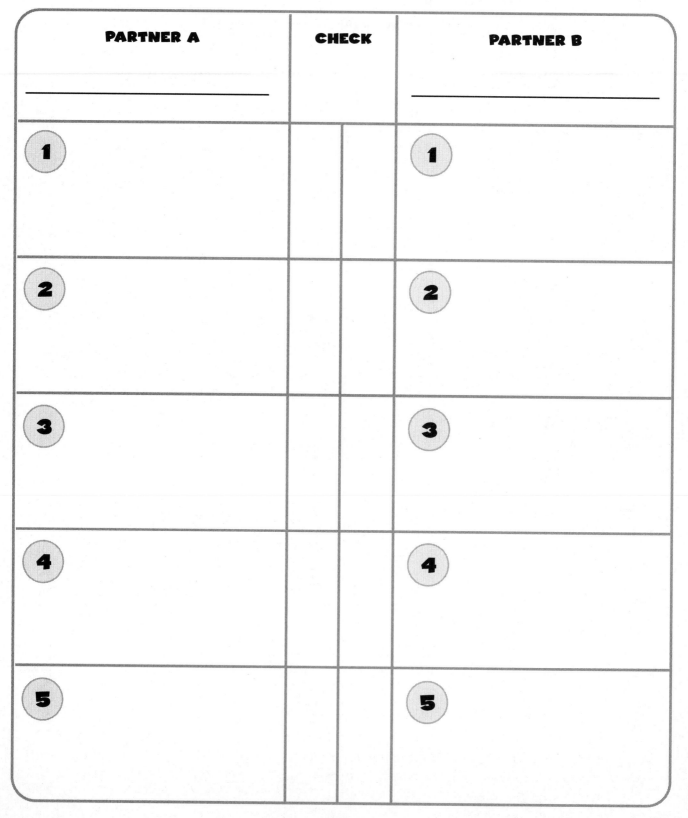

PARTNER A	CHECK		PARTNER B
_____			_____
1			1
2			2
3			3
4			4
5			5

Looping Game

Overview

Promote cooperative learning with this self-checking review game. Students in a group ask one another *"Who has…"* questions and respond *"I have…"* when their answer applies. If all questions are answered correctly, the person who started the loop also ends it with his or her *"I have…"* statement.

Before Playing

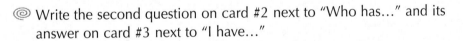

Looping Game Cards

I have: *1 kangaroo	I have: *4 cow
Who has: an animal that eats ants and has a long mouth/nose?	Who has: an animal that purrs and makes a good pet?
I have: *2 anteater	I have: *5 cat
Who has: an animal with sharp quills all over its body?	Who has: a small animal that people keep as a pet in a cage?
I have: *3 porcupine	I have: *6 guinea pig
Who has: an animal that produces milk and beef?	Who has: an animal that hops around and carries its young in a pouch?

1. Photocopy the Looping Game Cards sheet. (If you want more than six questions, make as many copies of the page as you need.) Decide on the topic you want to review, and write related questions and answers on the Looping Game Cards as follows:

◎ Write the first question on card #1 next to the phrase "Who has…" Then write the answer to this question next to the phrase "I have…" on card #2.

◎ Write the second question on card #2 next to "Who has…" and its answer on card #3 next to "I have…"

◎ Continue the process until you get to the last card. Write the question on the card next to "Who has…" then write its answer on card #1 next to "I have…" This ensures a loop.

2. Photocopy one set of the completed Looping Game Cards for each group of students. Cut the cards apart along the dashed lines. Place one set of cut cards in a plastic bag for each group and distribute the bags to each group. (Depending on how many cards you plan to use, each student may have one or two cards. I usually make sure each group has about 12 cards so that students are responsible for more cards and have to listen to every question.)

3. Read and discuss the Game Plan with the class to make sure everyone understands how to play the game. If playing this game for the first time, you may want to call on six volunteers to play the game as you guide the class through the directions.

Suggested Grouping:

3 or 4 players

You'll Need:

◎ Looping Game Cards (page 57)

◎ Resealable plastic bags (one per group)

◎ Game Rubric (page 42)

◎ Game Plan (page 56)

Looping Game
Game Plan

Objective
To ask "Who has..." questions and respond appropriately when a player's "I have..." answer matches the question.

How to Play

1. Assign a Materials Manager from your group to get the following items from your teacher:
   - bag of Looping Game Cards
   - Game Rubrics (one for each group member)

2. Sit in a circle with your group. Distribute the Looping Game Cards so that each student gets at least one card. Students can volunteer to take more cards if they like.

3. One player starts the loop by reading the "Who has…" question at the bottom of his card.

4. Look at your "I have…" statement to see if it answers the question. The player with the correct answer will read her "I have…" statement aloud. Then that player reads the "Who has…" question on her card.

5. Repeat step 4 until the player who started the loop ends it with his "I have…" statement. If this doesn't occur, somebody answered incorrectly during the game. Start over.

6. After your group has finished playing the game, have each member fill in a Game Rubric to evaluate the group's performance. The Materials Manager should return the bag of cards and rubrics to _____ .

7. Work on the following activity while you wait for all the other groups to finish playing:

_____

_____

_____

Looping Game Cards

I have:

Who has:

I have:

Who has:

I have:

Who has:

I have:

Who has:

I have:

Who has:

I have:

Who has:

Grab-a-Slate

Suggested Grouping:

Individual (some students may need a partner)

You'll Need:

◎ Slate for each student (e.g., piece of paper, mini chalkboard, mini dry-erase board, laminated piece of white construction paper)

◎ Erasers (e.g., tissue, chalkboard erasers, old socks, paper towels)

◎ Writing utensils (e.g., pencils, dry-erase marker, chalk)

◎ Lined paper (one per person)

◎ Game Plan (page 59)

Overview

Challenge students to work individually to answer review questions on a slate (chalk or dry-erase) and display their answer when you say, *"Show me."*

Before Playing

1. Decide on the topic you want students to review. Then write a list of important questions or problems along with an answer key. (I normally write 10 to 15 questions.)

2. If you feel the material may be difficult, have students partner up to do this activity. Otherwise, challenge students to play this game individually. By having students play individually, you can find out which students still need more help.

3. Read and discuss the Game Plan with the class to make sure everyone understands how to do the activity. As you play, take mental notes on who doesn't understand the concepts. Take time to reteach these students after the activity.

Grab-a-Slate
Game Plan

Objective

To answer questions or problems correctly on the slate and show it to your teacher for immediate feedback.

How to Play

1. Make sure you have a slate, writing utensil, eraser, and lined paper ready.

2. Listen carefully as the teacher calls out the question or problem. Write your answer largely and clearly on the slate and turn it over so that nobody can see.

3. When the teacher says, *"Show me,"* turn the slate toward her so she can see your answer clearly. The teacher will then call out the answer or show how to solve the problem.

4. If you are correct, put a tally mark in the upper right-hand corner of the lined sheet of paper.

5. Erase your answer on the slate. Repeat steps 2 through 4 until your teacher has asked all of the questions.

6. When all questions have been asked, write the following on the lined paper before turning it in:

    ◎ your name and title of review

    ◎ how many tally marks you received

    ◎ which concepts you had difficulty with

    ◎ which areas you need to study more

You're It!

Suggested Grouping:

6 players

You'll Need:

- ◎ You're It! Question Cards (page 62)
- ◎ Lined paper (for answer key)
- ◎ Resealable plastic bags (one per group)
- ◎ Dice (one per group)
- ◎ Sticky notes (one per person)
- ◎ Paper (one per group)
- ◎ Pencils (one per group)
- ◎ Game Rubric (page 42)
- ◎ Game Plan (page 61)

Overview

Students will answer review questions based on a number they are assigned. The team with the most points wins the game.

Before Playing

1. Photocopy the You're It! Question Cards sheet. (Depending on how many questions you want to cover, make as many copies of the page as you need.) Decide on the topic you want to review, and write related questions on the cards. Write the answers on a separate lined sheet of paper. Number the questions and answers so students can match them on their own.

You're It! Question Cards

In what galaxy is our solar system located?	How many planets are in our solar system?	What is the nearest star to our planet?
Name the gas planets in our solar system.	Name the rocky planets in our solar system.	Which planet is closest to the sun?
Which planet is home to the Great Red Spot?	How many moons orbit the planet Mars?	Which planet is farthest away from the sun?
Which planet rotates on its side?	What lies between the planets Mars and Jupiter?	Which planet has a very visible ring system?
Around which planet does the moon Europa orbit?	What is a meteor?	What is a comet?

2. Photocopy one set of the completed question cards for each group of students. Cut the cards apart along the dashed lines. Place one set of cut cards and the folded answer sheet in a plastic bag for each group.

3. Divide the class into groups of six students. (If your class doesn't evenly divide into six, you can either have extra students join other groups and share a number with one of the players, or have them start a smaller group and assign each player up to two numbers.)

4. Read and discuss the Game Plan with the class to make sure everyone understands how to play the game.

You're It!
Game Plan

Objective
Answer review questions when your number comes up on the die.
The group with the most points wins the game.

How to Play

1. Sit in a circle with your group. Assign a Materials Manager from your group to get the following items from your teacher:

- Bag of You're It! Question Cards with answer key
- Paper and pencil
- Game Rubrics (one for each group member)
- Die
- 6 sticky notes

2. Assign one person to be the Scorekeeper and give him the paper and pencil. Assign another person to be the Timekeeper. (The Timekeeper can use a stopwatch OR count to 15 in her head). When it's the Timekeeper's turn, the person next to her can keep time during the turn.

3. Hand each player a sticky note, then number off from 1 to 6. Each person writes his or her name and number on the sticky note and places it on his or her shirt.

4. To see which player takes a turn, roll the die. The player whose number matches the die draws a question card, reads it aloud to the group, and tries to answer it within 15 seconds. Check the answer sheet to see if the player is correct. If so, the team earns one point. The player puts the card in a discard pile and rolls the die to see whose turn is next.

5. Continue taking turns rolling the die and answering questions until all the cards have been drawn.

6. After your group has finished playing the game, have each member fill in a Game Rubric to evaluate the group's performance. The Materials Manager should return the bag of cards and rubrics to _____.

7. Work on the following activity while you wait for all the other groups to finish playing:

_____

You're It! Question Cards

For Teachers

Battle Bus

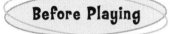

Overview

Challenge pairs of students to answer review questions as they try to locate their partner's Battle Buses hidden on a grid.

Before Playing

1. Photocopy the Battle Bus Question Cards sheet. Decide on the topic you want students to review and write related questions on the cards. Write the answers to each question on a separate sheet of lined paper. Number the questions and answers.

2. Photocopy one set of the completed Battle Bus Question Cards and answer sheet for each pair of students. Cut the question cards apart along the dashed lines. Place a set of question cards and the folded answer sheet in a plastic bag for each pair.

3. Photocopy the Battle Bus Game Sheet for each student.

4. Pair students or allow them to choose partners they want to work with. Distribute one bag of game cards and two Battle Bus Game Sheets to each pair.

5. Read and discuss the Game Plan with the class to make sure everyone understands how to play the game.

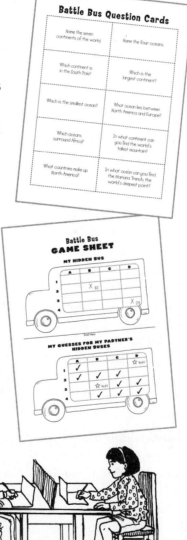

Suggested Grouping:

2 players

You'll Need:

◎ Battle Bus Question Cards (page 65)

◎ Battle Bus Game Sheet (page 66)

◎ Lined paper (for answer key)

◎ Resealable plastic bags (one per pair of students)

◎ Game Rubric (page 42)

◎ Game Plan (page 64)

Battle Bus
Game Plan

Objective

Locate your partner's two buses that are hidden in the Battle Bus Game Sheet grid. You can guess each bus's location each time you answer a question correctly. The first person to find both buses wins.

How to Play

1. Take a bag of Battle Bus Question Cards, two Battle Bus Game Sheets, and two Game Rubrics from your teacher.

2. Without showing your partner, mark an X on any two squares of the grid at the top of game sheet. These are your hidden Battle Buses that your partner will try to locate. Fold your Battle Bus Game Sheet in half so that the bottom bus lies flat on the desk, while the top bus stands upright. Place a book or folder behind your game sheet so your partner can't see through the paper. Sit facing your partner.

3. Stack the question cards within easy reach of both players. Keep the answer sheet in the plastic bag unless you need to check to see if an answer is correct.

4. Decide who goes first. Pick the top card in the stack and read the question to your partner. If your partner answers the question incorrectly, you can take

your turn. If he answers correctly, he can guess the coordinates of one Battle Bus. For example, he might ask, *"Is your Bus located in A4?"*

⊚ If he guesses correctly, say, *"You found the Bus!"*

⊚ If he guesses incorrectly, he should check the coordinate at the bottom of his game sheet as a reminder that A4, for example, is empty.

Place the question card in a discard pile.

5. Continue taking turns asking and answering questions, and guessing the location of each other's Battle Buses. The first person to guess where BOTH buses are located wins.

6. After you and your partner have finished playing the game, fill in the Game Rubric to evaluate each other's performance. Return the bag of cards and the Game Rubrics to

_____ .

7. Work on the following activity while you wait for all the other groups to finish playing:

_____

_____

Battle Bus Question Cards

Battle Bus
GAME SHEET

MY HIDDEN BUS

Fold Here

MY GUESSES FOR MY PARTNER'S HIDDEN BUS

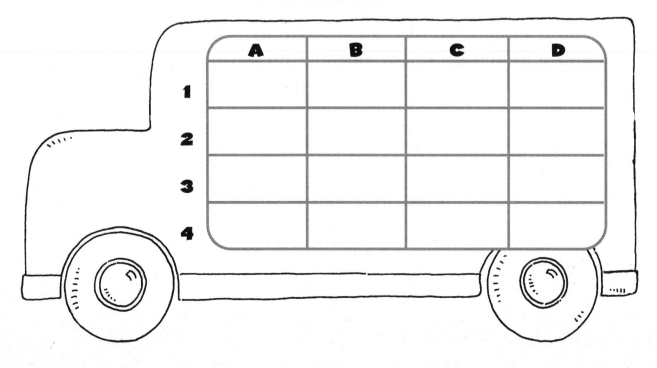

Dice-a-Rama

Overview

Get students revved up for review with this competitive whole-class game. Two teams compete against each other to score up to two points on each turn—the first point for quickly solving a math computation problem, the second point for correctly answering a review question. The team with the most points at the end of the game wins.

Before Playing

1. Decide what topic you want to review. On a sheet of paper, list 20 to 30 related questions and answers.

2. Divide the classroom into two teams, making sure both teams are of equal ability. Give each team time to come up with its own name.

3. Create a T-chart on the board, labeling each side with the team names. For example:

TIGERS | LIONS

As you play the game, keep score using tally marks. (Sometimes I have a helper tally the points for me so I can better focus on the questions and answers.)

4. Read and discuss the Game Plan with the class to make sure everyone understands how to play the game.

Suggested Grouping:

Whole class divided into two teams

You'll Need:

◎ 2 dice (If possible, get the large, soft dice that can be thrown on the ground for all children to see.)

◎ Lined paper

◎ Game Plan (page 68)

FOR STUDENTS

Dice-a-Rama
Game Plan

Objective

Work as a team to earn up to two points at each turn. Earn the first point by quickly solving a math computation problem using the two numbers you roll on the dice. Earn an extra point by answering a review question from your teacher. The team with the most points at the end of the game wins.

How to Play

1. Form two teams. (Your teacher will assign members to each team.)

2. Stand in line with your teammates. There should be no talking once the game begins. If someone on your team talks, your team will lose a point.

3. The first person from both lines steps forward and takes a die from the teacher. When the teacher says, *"Roll 'em,"* each student rolls a die.

4. When both dice stop rolling, the teacher will call out a mathematical function (i.e., add, subtract, multiply, or divide). The first player to correctly solve the math problem using the two numbers from the dice earns a point.

   For example, say a 3 and a 4 are rolled, and the teacher says, *"Multiply."* The first player to correctly call out 12 gets a point. If a player incorrectly says 7, for example, the other player can try to answer correctly and earn the point.

Dice-a-Rama
(continued)

5. The player who answered correctly can earn an extra point for the team by answering a review question read by the teacher. If the player answers correctly, her team gets another point. If not, the other player can try to answer the question. If he answers correctly, his team earns the point. Both players then move to the end of the line, and the next person from each line steps forward.

6. Repeat steps 3 through 5 to continue playing the game until all review questions have been asked. The team with the higher score wins.

POSSIBLE POINTS:

Scenario 1:	Team A	Team B
Dice Roll	YES	
Review Question	YES	
Total Points	2	

Scenario 2:	Team A	Team B
Dice Roll	NO	YES
Review Question		YES
Total Points		2

Scenario 3:	Team A	Team B
Dice Roll	YES	
Review Question	NO	YES
Total Points	1	1

Scenario 4:	Team A	Team B
Dice Roll	NO	YES
Review Question	YES	NO
Total Points	1	1

Plus/Minus Game

Overview

In this cooperative game, players earn points based on the roll of the dice. When a student answers a question correctly, the number he or she rolls gets added to the team's total score. Otherwise, the number is subtracted. The team with the highest total score wins.

Suggested Grouping:

3 or 4 players

You'll Need:

◎ Plus/Minus Question Cards (page 72)

◎ Plus/Minus Game Sheet (page 73)

◎ Resealable plastic bags (one per group)

◎ Dice (2 per group)

◎ Game Rubric (page 42)

◎ Game Plan (page 71)

Before Playing

1. Photocopy the Plus/Minus Question Cards sheet. (Depending on the number of questions you want to cover, make as many copies of the page as you need.) Decide on the topic you want to review, and write related questions on the cards. Write the answer in small print below the question on each card OR write the answers on a lined sheet of paper. Number the questions and answers so students can match them on their own.

2. Photocopy one set of the completed question cards for each group of students. Cut the cards apart along the dashed lines. Place one set of cut cards in a plastic bag for each group.

3. Divide the class into groups of three or four students. Distribute the bags to each group along with a Plus/Minus Game Sheet and two dice.

4. Read and discuss the Game Plan with the class to make sure everyone understands how to play the game.

Plus/Minus Game
Game Plan

Objective

Answer questions correctly and earn points based on a roll of the dice. The team with the most points at the end of the game wins.

How to Play

1. Assign a Materials Manager from your group to get the following items from your teacher:

- Bag of Plus/Minus Question Cards
- 2 dice
- Plus/Minus Game Sheet
- Pencil
- Game Rubrics (one for each group member)

2. Roll the dice to see who goes first. Play goes clockwise from the person with the highest dice roll. On the game sheet list each player's initials in the first column in the order that he or she plays.

3. To take a turn, roll the dice and add the numbers on the dice. Record the total on the game sheet under Dice Roll. For example, if you roll a 6 and a 2, write 8 under Dice Roll.

4. The person to the right of the player takes a question card and reads it to the player. If the player answers the question correctly, add his Dice Roll to the Total. If not, subtract his Dice Roll from the Total. Put the question card in a discard pile.

5. Continue taking turns, repeating steps 3 and 4, until all the question cards have been used up. Write your group's total score at the bottom of the game sheet.

6. After your group has finished playing the game, have each member fill in a Game Rubric to evaluate the group's performance. The Materials Manager should return the bag of cards, dice, game sheets, and rubrics to _____ .

7. Work on the following activity while you wait for all the other groups to finish playing:

_____

Plus/Minus Question Cards

Plus/Minus
GAME SHEET

Student Names: _____   _____

_____   _____

PLAYERS' INITIALS	DICE ROLL	CORRECT OR INCORRECT (C OR I)	POINTS SCORED	TOTAL
1				
2				
3				
4				
5				
6				
7				
8				
9				
10				
11				
12				
13				
14				
15				
16				
17				
18				
19				
20				

TOTAL SCORE _____

Create-a-Game

Suggested Grouping:

2 players

You'll Need:

◎ Cardboard, posterboard, or construction paper

◎ Markers, crayons, or colored pencils

◎ Scissors, glue, and any other supplies students may need

◎ Dice and other game pieces (e.g., buttons, dried pasta, coins)

◎ Information on the unit you want to review

◎ Create-a-Game Evaluation Sheet (page 76)

◎ Game Plan (page 75)

Overview

Encourage students to work cooperatively with a partner to create a fair game that gives a good review of information. Students will play each other's games when completed.

Before Playing

1. Since this game requires creativity, you may want to give students about four hours (or one to four class periods) to come up with a game.

2. Pair students or allow them to choose partners they want to work with. (You may decide to put students in groups of three, but I've found that when three are involved one person doesn't do as much work as the other two.)

3. Decide on the topic you want students to review. Assign students the chapters to review OR give students specific questions that must be included in the game. For example, you may instruct students to choose questions from Chapter 14 on the American Revolution or create problems related to fractions.

4. Read and discuss the Game Plan with the class to make sure everyone understands what to do. If possible, show students an example of a finished game so they become more motivated to do a better job.

5. When all the groups have finished creating their games, allow students one or two class periods to play and evaluate each other's games.

FOR STUDENTS

Create-a-Game
Game Plan

Objective
To create a game board that will help other students review important information.

How to Play

1. Create a game with your partner that meets the following requirements:

◎ Write 15 to 20 questions related to this topic: _____

◎ Write an answer key (on a piece of paper, making sure answers are labeled clearly)

◎ Design a colorful and creative thematic game board that is full of surprises and:

- can be played by at least three players;

- has a creative title;

- has a clear set of directions on how to play the game;

- has a way for players to move around the game board (e.g., dice, spinner);

- includes game pieces (e.g., dice, spinners, game pieces, cards) in a resealable plastic bag; and

- has an ending or goal clearly stated (for example, the player with the most money wins).

For example:

Content: Rain Forest

Jungle theme with monkeys, plants, grubs, and lions pictured on game board

Surprises: Lost in the jungle. Lose a turn. Quicksand! Sink back 10 spaces.

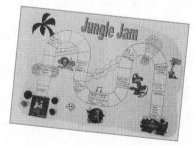

2. After you and your partner have finished making your game, write on a sheet of paper what you worked on and how you contributed to the game. On top of the page, write the title "My Contributions." This ensures that BOTH partners work equally on the game. Hand both your and your partner's sheets to your teacher.

3. On Game Day be ready to play and evaluate somebody else's game.
GAME DAY DATE: _____

Create-a-Game
EVALUATION SHEET

Game Makers: _____ **and** _____

Evaluators: _____ **and** _____

Directions: Rate each of the criteria below on a scale of 0 to 3. Write the score on the blank line before each criterion.

0 – Does not meet criteria at all

1 – Somewhat meets the criteria

2 – Meets the criteria well

3 – Goes above and beyond – SUPER job!

_____ Includes 15 to 20 questions related to this topic: _____

_____ Includes a clearly labeled answer key

_____ Has a colorful and creative thematic game board that is full of surprises

_____ Can be played by at least three players

_____ Has a creative title

_____ Includes a clear set of directions on how to play the game

_____ Has a way for players to move around the game board (e.g., dice, spinner)

_____ Includes game pieces (e.g., dice, spinners, game tokens, cards) in a resealable plastic bag

_____ Clearly states an ending or goal (for example, the player with the most money wins)

_____ We enjoyed playing this game!

_____ **TOTAL SCORE**

Compliments: _____

_____

_____

Suggestions: _____

_____

_____

25
STUDY SECRETS FOR STUDENTS

Here are some first-rate timesaving tips that will help you do your best
while studying for a test or quiz, or just while doing homework.

 1 Set goals ahead of time.
Make sure you know what you need to learn and why. (For example, *I need to learn the five causes of the Civil War to complete my project.*) Give yourself ample time to study the information. Plan when, where, and how you will study.

 2 Use a planner at school and at home.
On your planner, jot down each project or assignment, its due date, and the supplies (books or notebooks) you need to complete the assignment. After completing an assignment, place a check mark next to it. This helps give you a sense of accomplishment.

 3 Create a study area at home.
This study area should be free from distractions—no TV, loud voices, and so on. Keep all the materials you'll need (paper, pencils, pens, sticky notes, stapler, dictionary, thesaurus, etc.) readily available and within easy reach. Make sure you have plenty of light.

4 Organize your notes.
The simple act of organizing or rewriting your notes automatically transfers information from your short-term to your long-term memory. While you are rewriting and reorganizing your notes in a meaningful way, your brain is automatically reviewing it. Because you're organizing your notes in a way that matches how you learn best, you will most likely remember them better than if you just studied from the notes your teacher delivered.

 5 Assign yourself a study buddy.
Think of a friend from your class whom you can call with questions about assignments. Have the phone number nearby, but don't allow the phone conversation to take up valuable study time.

 6 Complete one assignment at a time.
If you move randomly from one study project to another, your brain will have a hard time keeping all that information straight and organized. Finish one project before starting another. Gather all the books, papers, and materials that you will need to complete the current assignment on your study table. Place all other materials on the floor until it's time for the next assignment.

 7 Each evening, create a realistic schedule to accomplish your tasks.
For example:
4:00 – 5:00 p.m.   soccer practice
5:00 – 6:00   relax/do chores/eat supper
6:00 – 6:20   work on research project

6:20 – 6:25	snack and water break
6:25 – 6:45	complete math homework
6:45 – 6:50	stretch break
6:50 – 7:10	study for quiz

8 Keep your study periods the same length.

If you alternate between long and short periods of study, you will remember less than if you divide your study time up into equal periods. For example, study for 20 minutes, then take a 5-minute break. Continue with this pattern until your assignments are completed.

9 Keep a positive attitude about studying.

Do you have an "I can" attitude? If not, free up your mind by writing down or discussing with someone what's stressing you out.

10 Fully concentrate on the material.

Avoid all distractions. Listen only to music that doesn't have words and turn off the television. The mind can focus only on one thing at a time.

11 Connect the information you're learning with past experiences and knowledge.

Relate the information to your life. Have you ever experienced something similar to what you're reading? How does the information you're learning relate to something you have learned before? Take some time to reflect on the topic.

12 Get actively involved with the information.

As you read or study, take notes, create outlines, draw pictures, create questions, or highlight key points. You'll stay on task more and remember the information better if you're physically doing something with it.

13 Use mnemonics.

If you're having a hard time remembering key facts, try to create a mnemonic to give it meaning and help you remember it. For example, to remember the five Great Lakes, think of HOMES—Huron, Ontario, Michigan, Erie, and Superior.

14 Visualize words into pictures.

When reading a book, try to picture in your mind what is going on in the story. You might visualize what a particular character or setting looks like. Visualizing improves comprehension and helps you add more details in your writing. In fact, your brain can remember visual information much better.

15 Ask yourself questions.

After you read the assigned material, ask yourself questions about it. This not only helps you remember information but also pinpoints those areas where your understanding or recall is weak.

16 Take breaks.

Take 5-minute breaks after every 20–30 minutes of studying. Research shows that taking regular breaks improves your overall retention. Each break must be a complete change from the study. Stand away from your desk and do some stretches or exercise to music.

17 Eat some brain foods.

Blood sugar rises after a meal and drops when you're hungry. If your blood sugar is too low, your concentration nose-dives and your memory blows a fuse. Eating sugary snacks raises blood sugar for only a short period of time, then leaves you worse off than when you started. Eat protein-rich foods such as peanuts, peanut butter and crackers, cheese, and yogurt to keep your brain—and body—on the go.

Keep a water bottle near your study area.
Water gives your brain a boost of energy. The oxygen in water feeds your brain. Sodas and juices actually make you even more thirsty.

 Relax.
Tension blocks memory. Here's a quick way to relax: Sit in a quiet, peaceful setting and take deep breaths. When you breathe in, your abdomen—not your chest—should swell out. You want to draw air into the bottom of your lungs.

20 **Don't study when you're tired.**
Tiredness plays havoc on your concentration, making it difficult to remember important information. If necessary, take a short nap or try some invigorating exercises. These activities can help boost your memory.

21 **Exercise.**
Believe it or not, exercise helps you remember information better and faster. When you exercise, you pump more oxygen into your brain. The best time to exercise is right before an important study period.

 Dream on.
Did you know that your brain-wave pattern while you're dreaming (in the REM stage of sleep) is very similar to your brain-wave pattern while you're learning? During REM sleep your brain is cementing what it has learned during the day and discarding what it doesn't need to remember anymore. Get plenty of sleep at night to reinforce what you have learned.

 Review, review, review.
Experts recommend the following review time for new information:

 After every 10 minutes of study, review your work for 5 minutes (read it again quickly, focusing on important points).

 Review the information for another 5 minutes one day after you studied it.

 Review the information for another 3 minutes at the end of the week, at the end of the month, and after six months.

This review system has been proven to increase retention by 500 percent. To review what you have read, reread the table of contents, the first and last paragraphs in each section, chapter summaries, and key words. Try to recall the meanings of the key words from memory.

24 **Review for a test or quiz by having an adult (or sibling) ask you questions.**
After studying, ask an adult or sibling to create questions that might possibly be on the test or quiz. See how well you can answer the questions.

25 **Celebrate your success.**
Plan a reward for yourself after the test. When you're excited about something, your brain produces the neurotransmitter noradrenaline, a memory-enhancing hormone. Possible rewards could include a favorite snack, extra time to play a video game or board game, visit a friend, play with a pet.

BIBLIOGRAPHY

Alkon, Daniel L. *Memory's Voice: Deciphering the Mind-Brain Code*. New York: HarperCollins, 1993.

Baumann, James F., and Edward J. Kameenui. "Research on Vocabulary Instruction: Ode to Voltaire." *Handbook of Research on Teaching the English Language Arts*. New York: Macmillan, 1991.

Bennett, William J. *What Works: Research About Teaching and Learning*. Washington, D.C.: U.S. Dept. of Education, 1986.

Brennan, Herbie. *Change Your Way of Thinking: Memory*. New York: Scholastic, 1997.

Caine, Renate, and Geoffrey Caine. *Making Connections: Teaching and the Human Brain*. Menlo Park, NJ: Addison-Wesley Publishing Co., 1994.

Dennison, Paul E., and Gail E. Dennison. *Brain Gym*. Ventura, CA: Edu Kinesthetics, 1992.

Fogarty, Robin. *Brain-Compatible Classrooms*. Arlington Heights, VA: Skylight, 1997.

Howard, Pierce. *The Owner's Manual for the Brain*. Austin, TX: Bard Press, 2000.

Hunter, Madeline. *Mastery Teaching*. El Segundo, CA: T.I.P. Publications, 1982.

Jensen, Eric. *Brain-Based Learning*. San Diego, CA: The Brain Store, Inc., 1996.

Jensen, Eric. *The Learning Brain*. San Diego, CA: The Brain Store, Inc., 1994.

Jensen, Eric. *Teaching With the Brain in Mind*. Alexandria, VA: ASCD, 1998.

Levine, Mel. *A Mind at a Time*. New York: Simon & Schuster, 2003.

Markowitz, Karen, and Eric Jensen. *The Great Memory Book*. San Diego, CA: The Brain Store, Inc., 1999.

Marzano, Robert, Debra Pickering, and Jane E. Pollock. *Classroom Instruction That Works*. Alexandria, VA: ASCD, 2001.

O'Keefe, John, and Lynn Nadel. *The Hippocampus as a Cognitive Map*. New York: Oxford University Press, 1990.

Parnell, Dale. *Why Do I Have to Learn This?* Waco, TX: CORD Communications, 1995.

Sousa, David. *How the Brain Learns*. Thousand Oaks, CA: Corwin Press, 2000.

Sprenger, Marilee. *Learning & Memory: The Brain in Action*. Alexandria, VA: ASCD, 1999.

Sugar, Steve. *Games That Teach*. San Francisco: Jossey-Bass Pfeiffer, 1998.

Sylwester, Robert. *A Celebration of Neurons*. Alexandria, VA: ASCD, 1995.

Wolfe, Patricia. *Brain Matters: Translating Research into Classroom Practice*. Alexandria, VA: ASCD, 2001.